Directing for the Stage

Directing for the Stage

Richard Williams

THE CROWOOD PRESS

First published in 2018 by
The Crowood Press Ltd
Ramsbury, Marlborough
Wiltshire SN8 2HR

www.crowood.com

British Library Cataloguing-in-Publication Data
A catalogue record for this book is available from the British Library.

ISBN 978 1 78500 379 0

Frontispiece
Bob Goody as Fagin in *Oliver Twist* at the Liverpool Playhouse, 2000.

Typeset and designed by D & N Publishing, Baydon, Wiltshire

Printed and bound in India by Replika Press Pvt Ltd.

DEDICATION

The book is dedicated to the memory of Alan Dossor, an inspiring and committed theatre director, who
touched the lives of all who worked with him.

ACKNOWLEDGEMENTS

I would like to thank the following for their help in preparing this book. My wife Joanna MacGregor for
patiently reading and correcting the text; Geraldine Cooke for suggestions with the text; designers Janey
Gardner and Jane Wheeler, lighting and projection designer Arnim Freiss, and computer designer Bart
Fiut for their superb technical and photographic help; photographers Carol Baugh, Mike Eddows, Tricia
de Courcy Ling, Alastair Muir, Huset Mydtskov and Nick White for their generous help with photographs.

CONTENTS

INTRODUCTION

MY OWN EXPERIENCE

I have had a career as a director that has now lasted for over forty years. Like everyone in theatre I've had a mixed bag of achievements and disappointments. I've directed over 200 productions and hope that my story and my observations can be of value to any younger persons embarking on this career. This book is intended to be a very practical guide into the profession but, more than many other jobs, directing is about personality and there are very many paths by which directors realize their productions. Some directors are highly practical in their approach, treating the process of rehearsal almost like a military operation; others are dictatorial in the Hollywood stereotype of the director. Some can be inspiring, although personally they are dreamy and vague characters; and others might treat the job as if it were a therapy session: sometimes for whom is unclear – whether the director him/herself or the cast. All I can do is tell it as experience has taught me.

From a very early age I was interested in performing, and when I left school I got a junior position at The Liverpool Playhouse as a student assistant stage manager at £1 per week, then under the directorship of David Scase, who had been a member of Joan Littlewood's company. Among the actors were Colin Welland (who later wrote the film *Chariots of Fire*), Lynda Marchal (later writing as Lynda La Plante) and Warren Clark. From David Scase I learnt about discipline and the wider social implications of theatre; from

Colin Welland I learnt about story telling because he had a wonderful store of stories, mainly about working-class life; and Warren Clark just exuded joy at being in the theatre at all.

After graduating from Manchester University with an English and Drama degree, followed by a postgraduate course at Oxford, I carried on acting with great enthusiasm, until I was faced with the dilemma of whether to accept a lecturer post at Lund University, Sweden, or whether to pursue a new role that had become available at the newly established Everyman Theatre in Liverpool. I applied for the position of publicity manager and, to my surprise, was offered the job, which secured my future in theatre. At the time, I didn't realize that The Everyman was soon to become the most adventurous and admired theatre company in the country. This was because the board of the theatre had just appointed a new artistic director called Alan Dossor. Over the three years I was there, I was able to combine my publicity role with acting in small roles on the stage, which gradually grew with the success of the company.

THE EVERYMAN THEATRE

The Everyman at this time (the early to mid-1970s) became a landmark company. After a disastrous opening season where the company delivered thirteen plays, twelve of which were premieres, and which attracted 19 per cent audiences, the emphasis changed and the company got into its stride. Actually the formula for what would be the company's subsequent success was already embedded in the second play of the first season. The play was called *The Braddocks' Time* by Stephen

OPPOSITE: Liverpool Playhouse. Originally built as The Star Music Hall. It was the first repertory theatre to own its own building. BART FIUT

Fagan, and told the story of the radical Liverpool MP Bessie Braddock and her husband Jack, who through the thirties to the sixties fought for social justice in the city. The play contained songs (generally rather plaintive in tone), was about a local topic and had an unashamed left-wing political perspective. These elements continued to be the strong ingredients that, in following productions, like John McGrath's two hits *Soft, or a Girl* and *The Fish in the Sea*, transformed the theatre's fortunes from a disaster to a national success story. This path led to the company's most commercially successful production, Willy Russell's play *John, Paul, George, Ringo and Bert*, which transferred to the West End.

In terms of stage directing and play selection, the clear lesson to be taken from that period is that a director with a clear and consistent policy will identify and mature the audience. People generally like to know what they are going to get for their money, and what they most enjoy is variation in detail. So, for example, in buying a ticket for a football match many things are predictable – the number of players on the pitch, the rules of the game, the length of the match and so on. However, the situation is very different in theatre. A ticket for, let us say, *A Midsummer Night's Dream* leaves very many unknowns. It could be a joyous comedy romp with fifteen actors, or four actors giving the play a dark interpretation without joy. The Everyman Theatre found that establishing the likely parameters of a show – local, musical, comical, political – identified and drew in a loyal and lively audience.

The phrase 'house style' isn't used much any more but it still very much exists. At Richmond's Orange Tree and The Finborough in Earl's Court you're likely to see a forgotten classic, which has been dusted down and given a new lease of life. The Lyric Theatre and The Young Vic in London tend to present plays for young adult audiences,

often with younger performers. The theatres outside London are having a more difficult time because financial constraints have resulted in fewer home-produced plays and, consequently, it has become more difficult to sustain a clear-cut policy.

Alan Dossor at The Everyman in the 1970s stood for the strong socialism of the time. This chimed well with the audiences in Liverpool, with its history of radicalism, which was at that time fuelled by the struggle against de-industrialization.

Richard III at the Everyman Theatre, Liverpool. Jonathan Pryce, right, as King Richard; Anthony Sher, third from right, as Buckingham. CAROL BAUGH

Dosser's imagination in planning a season of plays, his rigour in rehearsals in demanding precision and high-definition performances, and his recognition that serious intentions can often be best served through humour made him a constantly inspiring – though often intimidating – leader. He made very great demands, but left plenty of space for actors to find their own solutions. There were guest directors, but not many, because Alan was keen to make his mark and use the opportunity to both establish his style of theatre and to establish himself as an influential director. Here is another lesson: a director should always be busy, that way you can improve your own skills and avoid dwelling on either the triumph or disaster of the last production.

I enjoyed being busy doing both stage work and publicity, but I realized that acting involved quite a lot of waiting around. I don't mean between jobs because I was only working at the one theatre, but

even in that context there was still a lot of hanging about. It didn't sit well with me to be called for rehearsal, arrive on time and be told that it was running late so come back in an hour. Another lesson for a director: try not to keep the actors waiting in rehearsal or at auditions.

NOTTINGHAM PLAYHOUSE

One of the guest directors at The Everyman was Richard Eyre, who took over as artistic director at Nottingham Playhouse. He invited a group of the Everyman people to join him in Nottingham, myself included. I was doing the same combination of acting and selling the shows when I was invited to apply for a job at The Arts Council of Great Britain, as it then was. This involved visiting two, three or more productions a week, and talking to the directors and attending board meetings. After a year I realized what I wanted to do was to direct. I arrogantly thought I could do it as well as many of the people I had seen doing the job through my Arts Council visits. I met with Richard Eyre and asked him to consider my returning to Nottingham, but as his assistant director. Amazingly, and to my lifelong gratitude, he agreed. From him I learnt about directing.

I learnt very many things during the following three years. In no particular order:

• Directing takes time. Be patient.
• High-definition acting.
• Dealing with awkward actors.
• Pre-planning and organization.
• A light touch in rehearsal and trusting actors.
• A cinematic view of the stage picture.

From Nottingham I realized my ambition and subsequently got the job of artistic director, in succession, of Manchester's Contact Theatre, then to The Oxford Stage Company (now Headlong), The Unicorn Arts Theatre in London and then Liverpool Playhouse. I had a long spell working in the commercial theatre and the West End. Along the way I've worked in New York, Japan, the Philippines, Indonesia, Canada, the London fringe, opera in this country and abroad, commercial and subsidized companies and so on. The usual mix for most directors, I guess.

From this amalgamation of experiences I have written what I hope will be useful to others wanting to follow this interesting, sometimes frustrating, sometimes amusing, but highly creative path.

This book is intended for people at the start or in the early stages of directing. It is laid out very simply in chronological order – from a history of the director in drama, to gathering ideas for a play, through preparations with the creative team, auditioning, rehearsing, technical and dress rehearsals, giving notes to the cast, opening and closing nights. There are sections on other areas where a theatre director might work and, finally, a roundup of the options for formal training as a director. Where it seems useful I have given an hour-by-hour description of the director's responsibilities. I have based the descriptions of rehearsals on a three- or four-week full-time period. The reader will have to make adjustments depending on his or her timescale.

It is written with a view to helping a wide variety of people coming to directing – a student without professional experience, a professional actor who is directing for the first time, a director of an amateur theatre group, a teacher daunted by a school or college play, a directing student at a drama school, or a university student who is trying their hand at directing – and anyone else who wants to know about the role and responsibilities of this unusual, but rewarding, career.

I suggest you read it straight through to get an overall idea of the scope of the book, and then double back to specific sections as you need. Enjoy the book and enjoy directing!

OPPOSITE: Poster for *Trumpets and Drums* at the Nottingham Playhouse. BART FIUT

TRUMPETS & DRUMS

a comedy of soldiering and wenching in 18th Century England

by Bertholt Brecht

(adapted from Farquhar's `The Recruiting Officer' by Bertholt Brecht with music by Wagner-Regeny translated by Alan Brown and Kyra Dietz)

NP NOTTINGHAM PLAYHOUSE

Tel 45671   in repertoire from   APRIL 22

1

THE HISTORY OF THE STAGE DIRECTOR

Where did the stage director come from? Has there always been such a figure? How has the role developed? Who are the key individuals? What are the key developments?

A stage director should have, like a classical musician, a good understanding of the history of their craft. The director should know the history and the applied theatrical conventions of every period of drama, and the names and achievements of the main personalities of the twentieth and twenty-first centuries. The following list is by no means exhaustive, and a suggested reading list of plays is appended at the end of the book.

ANCIENT GREECE

In Ancient Greece, the birthplace of Western drama, the director, writer and actor were originally all the same person. The drama derived from dithyrambic rituals, which were the hymns sung and danced to in honour of a god. Drama began as the dithyrambic rituals surrounding the celebration of the god Dionysius – the god of wine, fertility and ecstasy.

Developing from religious ritual, tradition has it that the first actor/writer/director was called Thespis. Little is known about him, and there is no surviving play from him. However, he is considered to be the first actor and the English word for an actor, 'thespian' (not used seriously now, but applied

OPPOSITE: Mike Roberts as Scrooge, Tom Silburn as Spirit of Christmas Present in *A Christmas Carol* at the Haymarket Theatre, Basingstoke. ARNIM FRIESS

jokingly to an actor behaving in a 'grand manner'), is derived from his name. He is also credited with linking the chorus with the plot, establishing the idea of a leading character (the protagonist) and refining the masks worn by the actor to define the different characters he played.

The solo, male actor took on several different roles and made each one clearly identifiable by changing the mask of the character. Thespis revolutionized the scope of the drama by acting individual roles, in contrast to the singing and dancing of the chorus. Thespis is known because he won the drama competition in 534BC, and because Aristotle, and the statesman Solon, recorded their impressions of him. Solon asked Thespis if he wasn't ashamed of telling lies as an actor, saying such behaviour would one day infect everyday conversation!

The actors wore built-up shoes called *kotherni*, masks and body padding for playing female roles. The performances were in huge, outdoor amphitheatres with near perfect acoustics. Attendance at the drama festivals was the duty of all citizens.

The writer was also the director ('*didaskalos*' meaning 'teacher'). The writer Aeschylus later added a second actor, and Sophocles added a third. There are thirty texts of Ancient Greek tragedies, of which *Oedipus Rex* is the best known, and about twelve texts of comedies. There is no record of modern-day productions trying to recreate the single, double or triple actor system of the original, although the chorus is always presented in a variety of guises. In the production of *Oedipus Rex* at The National Theatre, the chorus were dressed as

Greek amphitheatre, built fourth century BC. Seating capacity an astonishing 14,000 and possessing near-perfect acoustics.

businessmen. The comedies are often too topical to be judged worth regular revival (although Sondheim wrote a version of Aristophanes' *The Frogs*), but the tragedies still form an important part of the Western theatre repertoire. Any director should investigate the plays for their contemporary psychological insight, powerful impact and economically direct plotting.

ANCIENT ROME

The Romans, as in many things, adopted and rather coarsened the basic principles of Greek theatre. One of the differences was that as the Empire became Christianized, tension grew between church and the stage. The writer Plautus created the notion of the comic stock character, such as the Boastful Soldier (*miles gloriosus*) or the Lustful Old Man (*senex amator*). These stock characters later developed into Commedia dell'Arte.

The tragedies of Greek drama became coarser and bloodier in the plays of Seneca, though it was these plays, not the more sophisticated Greek equivalents, that appealed to the early Elizabethan writers in works such as *The Spanish Tragedy* (Kyd) and *Gorboduc* (Norton and Sackville). In terms of the role of the director, there is nothing to add from the Roman experience!

Following the fall of the Roman Empire (AD476) there followed a period of about 500 years during which there was no drama in a form we would recognize.

While references are found to actors (*histriones*), jugglers, rope dances in nomadic tribes, remnants of Roman mimes, popular pagan festivals and rites, there is no formal drama.

Epic poems, like *Beowulf*, were recited and sung by troubadours (called *scops*), but these are the equivalent of our contemporary singer/songwriters (for example Bob Dylan) rather than dramatists or playwrights. And there is certainly no indication of a directorial influence.

MIDDLE AGES

The church had been in opposition to the recitation of pagan epics, but became itself the birthplace of the next stage of dramatic history – in churches. In the second-half of the tenth century small pieces of liturgical drama were introduced into church services as a teaching aid. The first was based on the Christian Easter story of the encounter by the three Mary's with the resurrected Christ, when He asks them, 'Whom are you looking for?' or in Latin '*Quem queritas*?'. The choir originally sang this antiphonally. The Medieval Mystery Play developed from a simple dramatization of key moments in the Christian calendar. At first these were performed inside the church but, in 1210, Pope Innocent III banned performance inside the church, and responsibility for these, by now very popular, dramas was taken on by the city guilds (unions or confraternities of tradesmen).

Once the guilds were involved it is certain that there was some sort of director. The staging was on a mobile pageant wagon or in a static formation of multiple stages. The staging was surprisingly elaborate. In charge of the operations were The Keeper of the Register, which was an important position and had extensive directorial control, and The Master of Secrets, who was in charge of the machines (secrets) – the special effects. The special effects included flying (angels), trapdoors (devils) and the Hellmouth (a monster through whose mouth the damned entered Hell). There is a rather wonderful illustration of a Mystery Play in rehearsal, with a director figure who has a long pointer, perhaps to indicate who speaks next or to prompt the performer into action! The cycle of Mystery Plays would begin at dawn with the first wagon touring the town stopping at chosen places and performing the creation story. A procession of wagons would follow the same route, while the audience remained in the same place. When it was dark, the final story, *The Last Judgement*, would be performed with flaming torches and the Hellsmouth. When I directed a much shortened version of the play cycle, I and the cast were struck by how very powerfully the plays spoke – even to a predominantly secular audience, especially the division of people at the end into the Blest and the Damned.

ELIZABETHAN STAGE

The theatre of the second-half of the sixteenth century and early seventeenth century was, perhaps, less like that of our own time than is generally thought. There is a temptation to make associations in Shakespeare with our contemporary events. As Jonathan Miller points out in his book *Subsequent Performances*, the semiotics, sociopolitical circumstances, theatrical conventions and questions of fashion would almost certainly, if we could time travel, make the original performance of *Twelfth Night* not only strange for us, but in many ways incomprehensible. Just because we can find so much to recognize in Shakespeare's plays, and by extension in the plays of his contemporaries, doesn't mean that everything about them is similar to our own conventions or ways of thinking.

As far as the role of a directorial figure is concerned the following observations can be made.

The companies of actors in Elizabethan theatre were semi-permanent and, as such, the actors would have established a strong sense of understanding and ensemble performing. Experienced actors working together would hardly need a director to arrange the positions on the stage (blocking). We know from those companies who now work together over a long period of time that stage positioning becomes a matter of generous common sense. In other words, the actors who are speaking take a more central position on the stage and give way to other actors on the stage, as necessary. Each actor would have a copy only of the lines the character spoke, and the cue line

to each speech. So the actors would be listening and receiving as if they had never heard them before, and actually they only just had! To a modern actor, expecting three, four or more weeks of rehearsal, this sounds simply hair-raising.

Given the intensity of the performance schedule and very short rehearsal times, and the local competition from the bear-baiting and cock-fighting, it seems likely there was less time and maybe less interest in details. The King's Men (of which Shakespeare was a member) presented eighteen different plays in twenty-two days at Hampton Court during Christmas 1603. Typically, the rehearsal period for a play would be under seven days, and that would include the daytime performances of other plays in the repertoire. It seems that sometimes the only rehearsal would be on the morning of the first performance. Because of the lack of reference to rehearsals, as we might know them,

Diagrammatic image of the Elizabethan theatre. Note the large thrust stage with the canopy over it. GREG FIUT

scholars have concluded that, in some cases, there would be no group rehearsal other than a run through on the day of the first performance. The actors, having just their own lines and the cue, would be expected to learn their part in isolation, whenever they could.

The theatre of this period would not have been weighed down with the demands of 'naturalism'. This requires close textual analysis and, generally, in contemporary theatre, involves an extensive exchange of ideas between the actor and the director. The Shakespearean drama is epic and poetic, and while it was acute in representing the observable behaviour of people, there was no Freudian or Jungian psychoanalysis, which is brought to bear (either consciously or unconsciously) in today's rehearsal room.

It is worth making a connection between the pageant wagons of the medieval mystery plays and the Elizabethan theatre of the Globe or the Rose, and suggesting that the Elizabethan theatre is basically an extension of a wagon parked in a balconied inn yard.

The Elizabethan theatre worked within certain conventions. Patrick Tucker's company, The Original Shakespeare Company, put on some very interesting performances in the 1990s using only 'cue-scripts'. This resulted in highly charged, concentrated performances. Tucker is convinced that the lines contain very many signals and indications to the actors as to the requirements of performance. In fact some actors would insist that 'actioning' (see Chapter 6) is redundant in Shakespeare plays because the writing tells the actor how to analyse the line and how to act the line.

Whether the author or the leading actor took a directorial role is uncertain. The process of preparing a play at this time is described in detail in Tiffany Stern's book *Rehearsal from Shakespeare to Sheridan*.

RESTORATION THEATRE AND BEYOND

During the second fertile period of dramatic writing, in the seventeenth century, the period of the Restoration (1660–1688), it is more certain that the author and/or theatre manager acted as the director of the play. Very important developments took place in the design of theatres and the presentation of plays. For a start, the two original Restoration theatres were housed in indoor tennis courts. These were rectangular and the stage took up nearly half the floor space. On stage, the bare Elizabethan platform was replaced by an acting stage

THE TERRIBLE EFFECT OF THE THEATRES ACT

The history of the English theatre in the eighteenth and nineteenth centuries centres on a number of outstanding actor managers. Starting with David Garrick, all of the leading actors are recorded as bringing a new and exciting realism to the stage. This is a very surprising idea when we see it recorded that Garrick, when playing Hamlet, had a special wig made, which he could activate so that the hair stood on end when he saw the ghost of Old Hamlet! Garrick was noted as having a conversational style – he made the most of death scenes.

The reason why it is the actor managers, and not the playwrights, who are noted in this period is that there are scarcely more than a dozen plays of note in the nearly 200 years between 1737 and the early twentieth century. This is because of the Theatres Act, which – among other restrictions on theatres – introduced the censor, which more or less dampened down exciting and controversial themes. The focus over this long period is on revivals of the classics or new plays, which are now forgotten. The writers of new plays, broadly speaking, self-censored themselves, in the knowledge that if they didn't, someone else would. The repeal of the Theatres Act in 1968 resulted in a huge tidal wave of new work from writers such as David Hare, Howard Brenton, Trevor Griffiths, Howard Barker, Adrian Mitchell and Caryl Churchill. This cascade of new writing continues in this country to the present day.

backed by a scenic stage with sliding flats and a vista stage beyond. With only a few changes, this is the basic proscenium arch layout of the majority of Western theatres today.

As for directing, we can proceed through the seventeenth and eighteenth centuries and see the same sort of arrangements: either a leading actor or theatre manager (and in many cases this was one and the same person) took on the responsibility of organizing the stage presentation of the play.

NINETEENTH CENTURY

Kemble and Macready were both outstanding actor managers of the early nineteenth century, but it was Kean who brought a development to the production of plays. Charles Kean (1811–68) was particularly noted for his insistence on authentic designs, both of costume and settings. His productions of Shakespeare were admired for their attempt to create an accurate historical look. This is the link with more modern production conventions.

MEININGEN COMPANY

The real start of theatre directing, as we know it now, came with the largely unknown Duke Georg II of Saxe Meiningen (reigned 1866–1914). He was passionate about the theatre, had seen the development of a more natural theatre in London and carried the process further with his own court theatre. From the 1860s to the 1890s, with his stage director, Chronegk, and an actress, Ellen Franz (later his wife), he pioneered a naturalness of delivery that was the starting point for the exciting developments of the twentieth century. The Duke was the designer, sometimes director and financier, of the company. He tried to bring everything on stage in a unified vision. The verdict on the Duke's company was that the conventional, flamboyant acting style of the period was still very much present, but the deployment of the crowds of extras (apparently as many as 200 in some productions) was highly disciplined and, importantly, gave individuality to the extras in the crowd scenes.

The company was not built around a star actor, but was more of an ensemble. There were recognizable rehearsals, where Chronegk would encourage the actors to understand the whole play and not just their own scenes. He would devote time to the overall look of the play, and investigate the meaning and emotional content of a scene, as well as pay attention to the historical references of the play. The Duke worked with his stage director and designer to create a style of theatre that not only employed an historical look, but that offered the performers what today we would describe as 'a world' to inhabit. This involved replacing painted backdrops with a three-dimensional stage setting. Together with detailed research of the historical period, the elements for the ground-breaking work of Stanislavski were laid down.

With the technological advances coming with the Industrial Revolution, theatre production became more and more complex. Lighting, gas and later electricity, enabled different lighting states and, consequently, required someone to organize it. Audiences had a growing interest in spectacle – shipwrecks, train crashes – and this also needed co-ordination.

ANDRE ANTOINE (1858–1943)

In France in the 1870s and 1880s, André Antoine carried forward the ideas of the Meiningen Company. With an emphasis on 'naturalism' his work was recognized as being another move away from the more bombastic acting legacy of the large theatres, which characterized early and mid-nineteenth-century European theatre.

Because the concepts of 'naturalism' and 'realism' are central to the changes in art in general, and theatre in particular, it is worth pausing here to define each of them.

In theatre the use of the word 'realism' refers to a play that is recognizable as a slice of everyday life, and not a theatrical confection. The issues the play discusses should be important and not trivial, and the action should be straightforward. It is distinguished from romanticism and the mythological. 'Naturalism' on the other hand refers to the influence that environment and background have on a character and action. It concerns the pressures and changes brought about by circumstances. So a play may be realistic and the performances naturalistic. In actual fact the two terms are now more or less interchangeable. These twin forces exercised immense influence on the theatre in the latter part of the nineteenth and early twentieth centuries.

Antoine was devoted to the idea of the fourth wall, i.e. the audience is eavesdropping on events in a room (or other location) the wall of which, nearest the audience, has been removed.

TWENTIETH CENTURY

Konstantin Stanislavski (1863–1938)

The star, the guru, the original! Although Stanislavski is popularly credited with the invention of the director, we should acknowledge, as he did, the debt he owed to the Meiningen Court Company. He watched their performances when they toured to Moscow in 1890.

Stanislavski's most celebrated association was with Anton Chekhov at the Moscow Art Theatre (founded in 1898). From the earliest part of his professional career, Stanislavski employed, and extended, the detailed research that he witnessed in the Meiningen productions. Documents, pictures, even travelling to locations associated with the play in question, formed an essential part of the preparation for a production. In addition, while studying Chekhov's plays, Stanislavski recognized that what people were saying did not necessarily represent what they felt. He understood what is called subtext. The story of the relationship between Chekhov and Stanislavski is intriguing and well documented.

Stanislavski's work, as the only systematic description of an actor's training, is described in very many ways. It is possible to think of his career as falling into three parts. In the early years he worked as an actor with good success. He was dissatisfied with what he witnessed of the conventional approach to acting, and moved onto directing in

Stanislavski – the originator of the first system for training actors. Subsequent actor training systems have been an extension of, or a reaction to, Stanislavski's pioneering work.

the middle stage of his development. His approach to directing was heavily research-based and, once he had done the research, the approach in the rehearsal room was rather direct and emphasized the externals of the process. So, for example, he was very strong on creating the *sound world* of the plays. Most importantly – in this period – he becomes aware of the implications of subtext. Following this middle period, he shifts the emphasis of his work from production to rehearsal. It is here he initiates his work on a systematic approach to acting. He recognized different types of acting: external performance, which can be thought of as copying or imitating actions and vocals; and internal or psychological, experienced or lived-through, the acting style he wanted to achieve with his system.

Stanislavski's 'system', when later in life he was persuaded to write about it, might seem complex, and is regarded by some as unnecessary. As we shall see with Brecht, it is important to look at Stanislavski in the context of the conventionally flamboyant, gestural style of the late nineteenth century. Indeed, it might be possible to suggest that as most acting now is governed by the Stanislavski approach, there is less need to teach it, as it is what most actors have grown up watching and absorbing.

It is an indisputable fact that some people have an innate talent to transform into a fictional character and don't seem to need any theoretical framework to achieve the most convincing performance. For others there is the danger of thinking that simply by obeying the rules, and investigating the character through the series of exercises, which comprise Stanislavski's system, the outcome will automatically be a convincing performance. But after the relaxation exercises, the application of the questions and everything else suggested about the character creation in Stanislavski's system, the actor still has to make the representation of the character his or her own, and add talent. (Stanislavski is discussed again in Chapter 3.)

It should not be overlooked that Vladimir Nemirovich-Danchenko, a close colleague of Stanislavski, took a major responsibility for setting up the Moscow Art Theatre with Stanislavski. Together they established what, at the time, was an unknown level of naturalism in their productions.

Max Reinhardt (1873–1943)

Reinhardt placed the actor at the centre of his productions, and many actors recorded how he managed to get the very best performances from them. He began by instigating a theatre/cabaret, which emphasized lightness and comedy. He directed *A Midsummer Night's Dream* in 1905 and released Shakespeare from the customary heavy, ponderous delivery of the text, common at the time. He was responsible for introducing the drama of Ancient Greece into the modern repertoire. He turned his attention to film and emigrated to the USA. His interest in *A Midsummer Night's Dream* was undiminished and he filmed it in the 1935 with Olivia de Havilland and Mickey Rooney.

Vsevolod Meyerhold (1874–1940)

Although he had been an actor in Stanislavski's company, Meyerhold disagreed fundamentally with his old boss. Stanislavski insisted on naturalism in the construction of the setting, in the realization of the sound effects, in the cut of the costume and, most of all, in the truth of the acting. Meyerhold was interested in quite a different set of theatrical skills: namely, the circus and street performers with the sense of mystery, sensation and delight they bring to their audiences. Clowns, acrobats, Commedia dell'Arte, Chinese and Japanese theatrical conventions, and all other popular forms of entertainment, produced for him the essence of theatre – playfulness.

He developed 'biomechanics', a system of scientifically inspired, mechanical, automatic physical moves, with which the actor produced physical movement to create emotion, in contrast to Stanislavski who demanded the internalized creation of emotion. In the absence of existing plays that conformed to his vision of theatre, he edited, re-wrote and reorganized plays. One of the leading poets, playwrights and actors of the Russian Soviet revolution, Mayakovsky collaborated with Meyerhold several times and was said to have written *The Bed-bug* especially for him. Again, in strict contrast to Stanislavski's realism, Meyerhold wanted giant ma-chine-like sets. His designs were like scaffolding and cranes, derived from the constructivist movement of post-revolutionary Russia, rather than the realistic interiors of the middle-class houses of Chekhov's plays in the hands of Stanislavski. It is probably true to say that the seminal work and methods of Mey-erhold and Stanislavski, in their different ways, have strongly influenced all Western theatre since.

Yevgeny Vakhtangov (1883–1922)

Inspired equally by Stanislavski and Meyerhold, the Vakhtangov approach was a synthesis of both ways of thinking about acting. He called this syn-thesis 'fantastic realism' and brought together the apparent divisions of reality and artifice, psychology and physical expression, theatricality and behav-iour. He used masks, music, dance and abstract costume, as well as close examination of the texts.

Michael Chekhov (1891–1955)

Regarded as Stanislavski's best student, Michael Chekhov developed a psycho-physical approach to acting. Chekhov evolved a series of movement dynamics that apparently focused on the externals of acting, but were intended to enrich the inner, subconscious life of an actor's character. His ex-ercises and theories aim for transformation and imaginative realization of a role.

Erwin Piscator (1898–1966)

Admired by Brecht, who respected and was influenced by Piscator's membership of the Communist Party, and his belief in satirical, political theatre, Piscator was an innovator in the staging of drama. He used film, moving stages, travela-tors and scaffolding, which was highly influential in both Europe and the USA.

Bertold Brecht (1898–1956)

When you look at Brecht's life in detail, you realize that whatever you can say about him, the opposite is more or less true as well. He declared himself a poet and gained fame or notoriety by composing an anti-war song, *The Legend of the Dead Sol-dier*. Winning The Kleist Prize as a young man, his early plays were in the expressionist style before he wholeheartedly embraced left-wing politics and Marxism.

There is a great misunderstanding about Brecht. He is popularly thought of as an agit-prop kind of writer and director. He is regarded as someone who insists on hijacking the audience's own ideas and imposing a way of thinking. In reality his aim was to get the audience to think about issues within the play, and relate those thoughts to issues outside. His writing and directing thrives on the complexity and contradictions of human behaviour.

Brecht thought the design of his plays was very important. He worked on detailed preparation with his designer, Caspar Neher, on a storyboard of the play. The finished set allowed space for the actors, gave an impression of period and place, while the aim was also to create lightness and beauty. One way of approaching Brecht, who remains a contro-versial figure in some places, is to think of him as re-introducing the conventions of Shakespeare's theatre into the twentieth century. The similarities between Brecht and Shakespeare are striking:

- No matter how we present Shakespeare's plays now, he had no fourth wall.
- Brecht uses narrators to advance the action; Shakespeare uses a chorus figure. Consider the similar functions of the singer in *Caucasian Chalk Circle* and the chorus in *Henry V.*

- Shakespeare introduces songs, as does Brecht.
- Shakespeare teases the audience with the notion that we know we are in a theatre watching a play. For example:
  - In *Twelfth Night* Fabian says, 'If this were played upon a stage now, I could condemn it as an improbable fiction.'
  - Hamlet, alone on the thrust stage of The Globe, which looked like a promontory and had a roof over it with stars painted on the underside says, 'it goes so heavily with my disposition that this goodly frame, the earth [The Globe Theatre], seems to me a sterile promontory [the stage], this most excellent canopy, the air, look you, this brave o'erhanging firmament [the roof], this majestical roof [the roof again] fretted with golden fire [the painted stars . . . '.

- One of the major thrusts of Brecht's ideas of theatre was that the audience would never forget they were in a theatre.
- Brecht is keen for the audience to know what happens next. Shakespeare only wrote one original play. Many educated audience members would already know the stories of *Comedy of Errors*, *Holinshed's Chronicles of Macbeth* and so on.

Aristotle in *The Poetics* described the theatre of the Ancient Greeks. This, amazingly, has remained the blueprint for how to think of theatre for the most of two and a half thousand years. This involved identification with the characters, whereas Brecht was attempting to create a more dispassionate theatre.

The differences between Brecht's theatre and Aristotelian theatre are summarized in the Table.

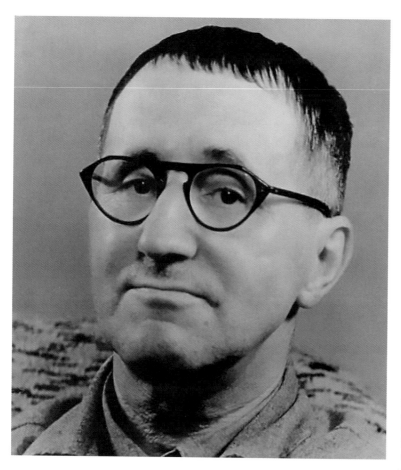

Brecht – his politically and socially engaged form of theatre led to a very different approach from Stanislavski's. Much of what he proposed is now embedded in our theatre practice.

Aristotle/Stanislavski v. Shakespeare/Brecht!

CONVENTIONAL THEATRE: ARISTOTELIAN	EPIC THEATRE: BRECHTIAN
Dominant, traditional, orthodox.	Dissident, subversive, resistant.
Theatre of illusion. Theatre of action.	Theatre of realism. Intellect.
Based on Aristotle's *Poetics*.	Based on Plato's *Republic*.
Models: Greek – Sophocles; Ibsen.	Epic tales of Homer, Dante.
Appeals to emotions and satisfies.	Appeals to reason and satisfies.
Psychological needs.	Intellectual needs. Objective.
Appeals to individuals. We relate, identify, feel empathy with the main character.	Appeals to the masses, moves us to action leading to social remedies.
No lasting consequences – emotions ephemeral.	A changed mindset, more permanent.
Suggestive, implicit, ambiguous.	Didactic, explicit, overt.
Interest in outcome of action.	Interest in course of action.
Emphasis on structure, causation, unity, cohesion.	Disconnected scenes, montage. Minimalism in props.
Assumes rational moral order.	Assumes chance. Nihilistic.
Affirmative sense of purpose. Fate controlled by Nemesis. Divine retribution, poetic justice.	Fate is chance. Random, chaos, absurdity.
Suffering is inherent in human condition. Leads to noble form of dignity.	Suffering is degrading, leading to brutalization and instinct for self-preservation.

The great legacy of Brecht lies not so much in his writings about theatre, such as the difficult and abstruse *Messingkauf Dialogues* – which have led to so many slow, dull, politically heavy, yet strangely politically naive productions – but the plays, the organization of a company as an ensemble and, most importantly, as a director, his redefinition of what theatre could legitimately discuss.

Antonin Artaud (1896–1948)

Although Artaud only produced one play in his lifetime, his thinking and writing about theatre was very influential. He wanted theatre to forget its preoccupation with psychology and his Theatre of Cruelty relied on elemental forces. The performance of *The Cenci* by Shelley was loud, windswept and spoken in a coded, non-verbal language – all aimed to shake the spectators from their conventional reactions. His work was the inspiration for Peter Brook's experimental Theatre of Cruelty season with the RSC in the 1960s.

Yuri Lyubimov (1917–2014)

A very influential Russian director who also acted, he rejected the label 'political theatre' and described his work as a search for ways of expanding the range of the use of space and style. His productions of *Crime and Punishment* and Shakespeare won accolades and awards. He drew together the influences of both Stanislavski and Meyerhold – his work was both realist and expressionistic.

Joan Littlewood (1914–2002)

The detailed history of Littlewood's career can be found in her effervescently readable autobiography, *Joan's Book*. Underestimated in her lifetime, and badly neglected today, she was the driving force behind Theatre Workshop, whose revolutionary production methods and philosophy set the pattern for much of what is commonplace in theatre today.

Joan Littlewood outside her theatre – The Theatre Royal, Stratford East. She had an unfulfilled ambition to establish a network of 'fun palaces' where people could sing, make pottery, learn about technology or just watch and listen.

Her politics were proudly left wing and she strongly believed in developing a theatre that was a clear alternative to the chic middlebrow, middle-class theatre of the 1930s, 1940s and 1950s. Following her training as an actor at RADA, Littlewood joined an agit-prop company, led by folk singer and writer Ewan MacColl, called The Red Megaphones, who played to working-class audiences, touring to industrial and factory sites in the north of England with short, sharp, often satirical political pieces. The group were inspired by the theatrical and political revolutions in Russia in the early twentieth century: Stanislavski, Meyerhold and the German Expressionists of the 1920s and, of course, Brecht. It is important to note that while many of the group's productions were necessarily new to meet the political situation of the day, the group also had an interest in the classical repertoire.

After the Second World War, Littlewood was the driving force behind reviving the group that had been The Red Megaphones. From 1945 she was the driving force of the group, which by then had become Theatre Workshop. The stated aim was to establish a genuinely popular theatre, which approached a wide repertoire of plays with a clear commitment to producing them with a left-wing sensibility. In the immediate post-war years, Littlewood developed her approach to directing. She was very interested in the physical presentation of character, and wanted her company of actors to be skilled in movement and singing, as well as acting. She had a commitment to making the spoken word resonate with comment on society. She wanted her theatre to be surprising, fun, critical of authority, multi-layered, experimental. Her productions were confessedly theatrical, that is to say she was happy to break the convention of the fourth wall, and to introduce songs into a production in defiance of strict naturalism. Like Brecht, her lively interest in new techniques included experiment with lighting and sound.

Her working methods put improvisation, allied with movement, at the heart of the rehearsal process. She insisted on rigorous research and on a collective way of working, which extended into equal pay for everyone in the company to collective working methods in rehearsal. Littlewood's methods were strange and unfamiliar to most actors at the time, and did not suit actors who were not used to it. However, it is easy to see now the resounding success of her pioneering work.

In 1954 she took up residence at the then disused and partly derelict Theatre Royal in the east London borough of Stratford. Here she initiated a wide-ranging repertoire of the classics, both period and modern: Chekhov, Sean O'Casey, Bernard Shaw, Brecht and Shakespeare. Her book contains a reading list for the theatre, which any director would benefit from. Her new plays included *The Quare Fellow* and *The Hostage* by Brendan Behan and the most celebrated of her devised plays with music, *Oh, What a Lovely War*.

Giorgio Strehler (1921–97)

The Italian director established the Piccolo Theatre, Milan, where he championed the work of Pirandello and Goldoni among other Italian writers. A socialist and keen director of Brecht's work (they became good friends), he more or less established, for the first time, the role of director in Italian theatre. He directed much of the classical repertoire, including Shakespeare. His productions were described as vibrant, precise and fresh. An actor as well as a director, he also produced opera.

Peter Brook (1925–)

Brook left Oxford University with the intention of becoming a film director but instead became one of the key figures in, first, British theatre, and then in French and European theatre. He is a director who likes to surprise with overt theatricality. His influences are Grotowski, Joan Littlewood, Artaud, Brecht and Meyerhold. He has great interest in improvisation in rehearsal and spends a long time preparing and rehearsing his productions. He believes the creative heart of the theatre is the actor and that the director is almost a facilitator. His range of productions is impressive. Beginning with his early, eye-opening revivals of Shakespeare – restoring *Love's Labour's Lost* was one of his great gifts to the theatrical repertoire – to one of the most influential productions of the mid-twentieth century, *The Marat Sade*, which grew from his experimental Theatre of Cruelty Season, to his journey through Africa performing *A Conference of Birds* with a carpet for a stage, to his farewell to the British stage with the circus-inspired *A Midsummer Night's Dream*, he has spent a lifetime searching for the essence of performance and the essential theatre language. He believes that art aims to open the everyday to reveal the mysterious world beyond. He moved to Paris where the French government awarded him the kind of funding he could not get in the UK. He toured the world with his largest production *The Mahabarata*. For all other directors, his curiosity, versatility and willingness to reinvent himself and his methodology should be an inspiring example. He has written several books on his ideas about theatre and there are many books and articles about him.

Sir Peter Hall (1930–2017)

After Cambridge, Hall made his name by directing the English premiere of *Waiting for Godot*. In 1960 he transformed the Shakespeare Memorial Theatre into The Royal Shakespeare Theatre and directed one of its most memorable productions, *The Wars of the Roses*, in 1963. This was regarded as one of the most significant Shakespearean events of the century. He left the RSC to become the director of the National Theatre. While Hall did not establish any particular methodology as a director, he was widely regarded as a visionary in his choice of repertoire and a highly skilled operator in the politics of the theatre world.

Ken Campbell (1941–2008)

Ken Campbell is a much-overlooked director, funster and practical joker. It is worth including him in this list because his peculiar, anarchic spirit brought delight and surprise to audiences in the UK from the 1970s into the twenty-first century. He rejected what he called 'brochure theatre': the long-term planned productions with well-behaved and fully trained actors, performing new plays or revivals of the classical repertoire. His choice of material for plays ranged from science fiction, through gothic horror, to wildly improbable re-imagining of well-respected plays – respectively, *The Illuminatus Trilogy*, *Charles Dexter Ward*, *The War with the Newts* and *Macbeth* performed in pidgin English. Campbell trained at RADA but was quickly impatient with the respectable middle-class theatre and took off with a company of like-minded actors to produce Shakespeare in impromptu performances in pubs, along with circus turns and Victorian fairground entertainments. He explored the byways and side-roads of theatrical performance, including a twenty-two-hour epic called *The Warp*. What any director can valuably copy is, first, his insatiable curiosity and unmitigated sense of fun – so that he could swoop between plays about Jungian synchronicity and Ancient Egyptian ventriloquism, and find connections – and, second, a rejection of all forms of theatrical snobbery. For him Shakespeare and Chekhov did *not* sit at the top of a hierarchy of worthy authors, but everything in the world was possible material, and everywhere was a possible performance space. He called his audience 'sensation seekers,' and his strongest note to actors was, 'act better!'

Mike Alfreds (1934–)

Described by Ian McKellan as one of the three best directors in the country, he is dogmatic in his

belief that instinct alone is not enough. He worked on publicity for film and studied theatre directing in the USA. His training there was rigorous, including analysis of painting, model-making, building scenery and publicity.

His own company, with one of the best names ever invented for a theatre company, Shared Experience (best, because that is what a theatre show should be), did away with scenery, costume and lighting to place the emphasis on the actor. His work with Shared Experience has often been in the adaptation of classic works of literature such as *The Arabian Nights* and George Eliot's *Mill on the Floss*. His method concentrates on the environment and space within which the action takes place, on the characters' relationships and the subtextual meaning of the play. He is avid about research and close examination of the text. He first achieves complete familiarity of the text. At the same time, the actors have to understand and create the physicality of their roles, because he wants the actors, being so free with what they know about the characters and the play, to be able improvise in performance – not the lines of the play, but the emotions and the staging. He works with a small number of actors who appreciate the freedom his approach allows them. He is critical of the conventional approach where the actors have to contend with sets and costumes in the last few days before the production opens.

Declan Donnellan (1953–)

Founder of the now internationally renowned company Cheek by Jowl, Donnellan remarks on two aspects of rehearsing. Having first auditioned carefully and exhaustively, he will give an instruction to the actor such as 'come from stage right.' The actor will comply but might have a good reason to suggest that entering from stage left would be more satisfactory. Donnellan will agree as he was only giving a confident start to the rehearsal. In this respect, the sensitive and intelligent actor almost directs him or herself, and the director, as one part of the job, is the editor of the possibilities discovered in the rehearsal. His second approach, which is the subject of his book, *The Actor and the Target*, is that the actor needs to focus on a target. The target can be an object or it can be a person, but it is crucial that the focus of the actor is not on his or her character's internal desire, but on responding to the object or person – the target. The target is a means of getting rid of the blocks, which inhibit the actor from doing what should come naturally – playing and acting – blocks that prevent a convincing performance. The repertoire of the company is very heavily inclined towards the classics. Often the cast are seated onstage throughout the performance.

Katie Mitchell (1964–)

Katie Mitchell's approach is to be very prepared before the rehearsal starts. Not so much deciding how exactly everything in the production will look and sound, but being sure that the director has got a solution to everything in the production, very much expecting that the work in the rehearsal room will provoke more interesting discoveries and solutions. At the start of her career she would ask questions to encourage the actors to follow certain lines of discovery, but finding this a very inefficient use of time, has developed an approach by which the actors are given a series of statements of imaginary situations, 'Let's say the date is . . .' and a series of specific circumstances, which are applied to the scene. Her directing philosophy is that the director gives very specific, local instructions and the actors 'do'. Although it sounds inflexible, in practice the actors benefit from having the confidence that the director has imagined the play in close detail from their point of view. She has tended to work with a smallish group of actors.

Thomas Ostermeier (1968–)

Thomas Ostermeier is a German director who has made an international name for himself by his stark productions of plays showing the reality of life on the margins of society. Opposed to the fashionable nihilism of some theatre practitioners, he underlines the need for unity and design in productions. His productions are strong on narrative and physicality, and he is a traditionalist as far as text goes, although he is happy to intersperse classical text with contemporary references, or even to stop the action completely to engage in a live debate with the audience, as happened in his production of Ibsen's *The Enemy of the People.* In his productions emotion is rooted in concrete, physical action. The name given to his genre of theatre is 'capitalist realism', which does not pull its punches in exposing the greed and violence caused by late capitalism.

IN CONCLUSION

From this selection of the history of directing and methods of some influential theatre directors, it is clear that the aims of the directors are very similar. With few exceptions the director wants to find ways to make the play text come alive when embodied by the actor. The director wants to achieve something that is called, and recognized when it is seen as, 'realism' but that is very hard to define.

In my own research, one of the noticeable comments by observers of the great actors of history, is that all those actors apparently portray their characters with exceptional 'realism'. Clearly the realism cherished by each generation of directors and actors alters with time. There are no absolutes. What we today praise as sublimely accomplished performances will, no doubt, seem strange, oblique and unconvincing sometime down the line. Yet another reminder that the theatre experience, if not the text, is written on the air.

Another theme is to deliberately run counter to realism and encourage the audience not to be seduced by the action, but to be moved to think about what they are witnessing.

The director does not need to follow a particular method, but by being familiar with the history of the medium will draw on the best approach in each circumstance.

2
THE ROLE OF THE DIRECTOR

TOWARDS A DIRECTORS' THEATRE

Stanislavski as Part of the Nineteenth-Century Tradition

The previous chapter outlined how the position of director emerged in the late nineteenth century and early twentieth century. Although Stanislavski was not the first to create the role in the way we now recognize it, he remains the towering influence because he wrote about his directing, as well as creating a systematic approach to acting.

The descriptions he wrote of how he wanted Chekhov's plays to be staged are very close to nineteenth-century traditions. So, in correspondence with Chekhov about *The Cherry Orchard*, Stanislavski is enthusiastic about the scenery, which he describes as containing a little chapel, a ravine, a stream, a manor house, telegraph poles, a puff of smoke to indicate a passing train, fog, and the sound of frogs and corncrakes. A review of a production by the English director Beerbohm Tree reveals the excessively realistic scenic effects, which are today thought of as laughable:

> For the second act – a boating scene – a river of real water was let into the stage of the theatre, to Herbert's intense and almost childish appreciation. A wonderful effect ensued. How he loved to try and bring woods and streams and founts and skies and mountains on to the stage! And pillared palaces, and long-drawn aisles: stately castles, grim battlements, battlefields, pine forests, beech woods, fields jewelled with daisies, and yellow sands!
>
> (Spectator Archive 30 October 1920 review of *Lady Tree's Biography of Tree*)

We can detect immediately that Beerbohm Tree's widow displays a real sense of wonder at this achievement. Before we get too reverential about Stanislavski, we must put him in a tradition of

OPPOSITE: *Hamlet* at Elsinore Castle with David Thelfall as Hamlet. RIGMOR MYDTSKOV

SOME OF THE ATTRIBUTES A DIRECTOR SHOULD POSSESS

- An ability to express him- or herself both orally and in writing, and to be creative, persuasive and prepared to take artistic risks.
- Excellent negotiation and interpersonal skills.
- Self-motivation and the ability to motivate and inspire others.
- Team-working and time-management skills.
- Awareness and understanding of technical issues, the workings of a theatre and the process of performance and acting.
- Ability to develop innovative ideas and to solve problems creatively and practically.
- Organizational and research skills.
- Knowledge of the requirements of the relevant health and safety legislation and procedures.
- Dedication and enthusiasm.
- A sense of fun – perhaps the most important!

nineteenth-century actor-managers who tried to bring the world on to the stage in a very literal way. However, he did listen to Chekhov, perhaps grudgingly, and began, perhaps, to recognize that the stage is a metaphorical place for the imagination to flourish, and not an empty space to fill with the stuff of the external world.

There is a frequent comparison made between the development of the theatre director and the emergence of the orchestral conductor. In the nineteenth century, as the Industrial Revolution gathered pace, cities expanded (London's population grew from 1 million in 1800 to 7 million by the of the century) and, consequently, both the theatre and the concert halls got bigger – more audience, larger stages, more performers – hence the need for someone to be responsible for coordinating and liaising with the increasing number of people involved.

It is from this world that Stanislavski emerges, but we have to understand that his real innovations were not to do with his direction, but his discoveries of how an actor can improve his relationship with the text of a play. That said, the director must know about Stanislavski and his work, because the actor and director are symbiotically linked to each other through his ideas. Actors will often refer to Stanislavski.

A REACTION AGAINST THE DIRECTOR

In the second part of the twentieth century there were a few voices raised against the apparently increasing importance of the director. Simon Callow, in his autobiographical book *Being an Actor*, takes a swipe at what he describes as 'director-dominated theatre'. (His updated version draws a gloomy picture of current British theatre.) However, he clearly adjusted his views because he went on, only a few years later, to start directing with the same great success that he achieved as an actor.

In 1972 a new national touring company was established by a group of well-known actors, which was called The Actors' Company. Among the original group were Ian McKellen and Edward Petherbridge. The philosophy of the company was that there would be no directors and no star performers, and the central idea was that the company would share lead roles and the directorial responsibilities. Essentially it was an attempt to return to the Elizabethan model of a self-contained troupe of actors among whom were the writers, directors and producers. The success of the company was its undoing, because as the company became more successful, its members became better known and other offers came in.

Mention should also be made of the actor Kenneth Branagh who established the Renaissance Theatre Company. There was a director for each production, but usually an experienced actor – Judi Dench, Richard Briers and Geraldine McEwan did that job.

As we have seen, for the majority of the history of drama there has been no director. However, all research indicates that someone took charge – whether it was the writer (as in the drama of Ancient Greece), the leading actor, or the producer or the owner of the theatre (as in the Restoration period). There is little or no evidence of a free-for-all in rehearsals.

A CHEEKY JOKE – IN THE BEST POSSIBLE TASTE!

There was a gently satirical joke that went round theatrical circles about The Actors Company. Allegedly, a local radio station was interviewing one of the company. The interviewer was keen to let the actor explain in detail how the company operated. He asked, 'How exactly does this policy of the company work?' to which the actor replied, 'Well, we all share the different parts'. 'But how does that actually work?' repeated the interviewer. 'Well, take for example Ian McKellen. This week he's playing Hamlet in *Hamlet*. Next week he's just playing the Second Footman.' 'Oh I see,' said the interviewer. 'And what is the play next week?' '*The Second Footman's Story*,' replied the actor.

There is one very important development in the progress of the director that should be noted. From the 1960s onwards, a kind of celebrity director has emerged. A regular theatre-goer, who is averagely informed, would probably find it a challenge to name any theatre directors of the 1930s, 1940s or 1950s who were not already established as actors, such as Laurence Olivier and John Gielgud. However, just issue the same challenge, changing the period from the 1960s to the present day, and many theatre goers would have no problem in producing a list, which might well include Peter Brook, Peter Hall, Trevor Nunn and Peter Stein. In addition, and more recently, the names of Ivo van Hove or Katie Mitchell are far better known than the actors who have featured in their productions.

The emergence of a 'director's theatre' caused a great deal of controversy in the 1980s because of the fees some celebrity directors were able to demand. Peter Hall and Trevor Nunn, in particular, were accused of making excessive amounts of money by using their positions in subsidized theatre. There was also a feeling that theatre was being subverted, and that an actor's medium was becoming the domain of a brand of show-off directors. Two other forces fuelled the idea that theatre was becoming less an actor's medium and more a director's playground.

One was the influence of continental European directors. In the UK there is a tradition that respects the language and the cultural legacy of Shakespeare. In Europe, and particularly in Germany, the cultural legacy flows from a different source. This seems to have produced a sort of freedom, or even irreverence, which permitted directors to take risks and invent eye-catching transformations of classical works. The other source was the reinvigoration of classical opera, both in the UK and abroad. Opera companies, in particular, from the 1970s onwards felt the need to modernize and appeal to a younger audience. One of the results of this trend was a revolution of the way the operas were staged. Because the overwhelmingly important aspect of opera for its audience is the quality of the singing and music, directors had a

freer hand with the staging of the works. Some of the wild invention in the opera world flowed back into the theatre as many directors, like Tim Albery, David Pountney and Jonathan Miller, worked in both media. The effect of this has been for directors to hold a more pivotal role in theatre than previously, and for them to be increasingly audacious in their production ideas.

SPECIES OF DIRECTORS

There are almost as many approaches to the job of directing as there are directors, which is not surprising when you consider that directing is about leadership, vision, inspiration and imagination. There is no fixed pattern and it is to a great extent a question of individual character. That said, there are certain categories we can distinguish.

The Director as Dictator

The director of popular imagination, fed by the image in many movies, is that of the director as dictator – shouting, gesturing, misunderstood, a diabolic genius. If only the director could be like that! The fictional Lermontov in the film *The Red Shoes* is this type, based on the very real Diaghilev. This type of director is constantly in a bad temper because nothing goes right according to his (and it is always a man) perfectionist mindset, and no-one is good enough to create the performance his fiery imagination has dreamt up. However, just because it is a popular cliché doesn't mean it doesn't exist. In real life there'd have been very many directors who ruled the rehearsal room with a rod of iron. They might have everything worked out in advance, or they might just as likely have complete faith in their own inspiration. John Dexter was a director who took no prisoners, but a glance at his achievements immediately shows the results were exceptional. Among his very many credits were *The Royal Hunt of the Sun*, *Equus* and *Othello* with Olivier. The problem with this type of director is that you have to be right, and bring in great reviews and full houses. With positive responses, a huge amount can be forgiven. A combination of being bad tempered in the rehearsal room followed by poor response from the press and empty houses are not the ingredients for a long career.

The Director as Martinet

The director as martinet is a subspecies of the family of director as dictator. This type of director will have worked out in close details how he wants the production to proceed. There will be close, detailed notes on entrances and exits. Every move of every character will have been planned in advance. The details of every relationship will have been decided and this director's script will be covered over in pencilled notes. This level of attention to detail is very positive in as far as the actors can feel safe, but they will also feel restricted. It can be a very good starting point but it doesn't create a positive, creative environment. It is often due to the director feeling insecure himself and is frequently witnessed in the rehearsals of younger, less experienced directors. No names!

The Director as Therapist

When Stanislavski first put his ideas together in the form of a system, he attached importance to the process of an actor accessing his own memories – especially memories that carried a strong emotional charge. By drawing on the actor's own reservoir of experience, s/he could then come closer to creating the right emotion for the character in the play. This is a concept Stanislavski rowed back from in his later writing, but it is one that his pupils-cum-acolytes in the USA wholeheartedly embraced. Stanislavski's 'system', a suggested way of approaching the creation of a character, was turned into 'the method', a prescriptive approach, which put particular emphasis on the idea

METHOD OR MADNESS?

There is a well-known, amusing story concerning Dustin Hoffman and Laurence Olivier when they were both filming *Marathon Man*. The scene required Hoffman's character to appear tired and dishevelled, having not slept all night. Hoffman (who attended The Actors Studio) stayed up all night and ran round a park, arriving on set exhausted. Olivier asked him why he looked the way he did, and when Hoffman had explained, Olivier said something along the lines of, 'Oh dear. We have something in England called acting!'.

of 'emotional memory'. Lee Strasberg, in particular, practised this when he ruled over The Actors Studio. With actors reaching back to find the emotional charge they felt when some very important event happened, the person who has instigated this exercise, the director, is the natural shoulder to cry on when the tears well up in remembering the death of a family member, or the anger when a friend betrayed a secret. In this case the director can easily think of him/herself as a therapist, healing some long-lost injuries. The truth is that very few directors are trained therapists, and raising strong emotions without the knowledge of how to safeguard the resulting effects is simply irresponsible. Don't do it!

The Director as University Lecturer

In the nineteenth century, acting was handed down father to son in a totally prescriptive way, which resulted in a predominantly 'exterior' style of acting, where gestures and physical expressions were the key to good performance. Stanislavski tried to bring order and naturalism to directing, growing in part from research. Indeed, Stanislavski visited Venice when he was preparing a production of Shakespeare's *The Merchant of Venice*. This detailed search for the authentic is still a key component in the preparation of many productions. Anthony Sher describes a visit to France in preparation for his performance in the title role of *Cyrano de Bergerac*. (He even carefully noted the variety of noses in France, because the length of his nose defines the character Cyrano!) The internationally famous director Katie Mitchell places enormous emphasis on research, both by herself and by her actors. In her case it has produced very many great productions, but it is important to remember that research is part of a process and not an end in itself. The director must remember – whether s/he has been to university or is an autodidact – that the rehearsal room is not the place to give long lectures. It is a place of *doing*.

The Director as Activist

This brand of director was easily recognized in the 1960s and 1970s. Director and writer John McGrath founded 7:84 Theatre Company, so called because (according to *The Financial Times*) 7 per cent of the British population owned 84 per cent of the wealth.

With a mixture of agit-prop and community-embracing productions, he made direct, incisive political drama aimed at changing the audience's mind on current social and political questions. *The Cheviot, The Stag and The Black, Black Oil* was an impressive hit in Scotland in the early 1970s. Other directors set

Scene from Brecht's *Good Soul of Szechuan* at the Platform Theatre, London. This production was staged at the time when libraries were being closed down. The production was set in a semi-demolished library. Tweets were projected during the action.
TRICIA DE COURCY LING

MAN FRIDAY
adrian mitchell

Music by Mike Westbrook, performed by 'Solid Gold Cadillac'

7% of the population of this country owns 84% of the wealth.

7:84
THEATRE COMPANY

up companies with similar viewpoints. Among the most prominent were Belt and Braces, Monstrous Regiment, Gay Sweatshop and Red Ladder. Some of the work was devised and some was text-based, such as Dario Fo's *Accidental Death of an Anarchist*. This type of director must watch out that politics do not eclipse the enjoyment. McGrath's success was partly because he could write and direct good jokes.

The Director as Believer in Chance

There is another breed of director altogether who relies on chance. Geoffrey Reeves was this kind of director. He had been an assistant to Peter Brook and carried with him a generous *laissez-faire* approach to theatre production. It was said that he had absent-mindedly cast two actors for the title role in the same production of *Hamlet*. Realizing his mistake as they both arrived on the first day for the read through, he quickly rationalized the situation by saying he had wanted to have them both, and the idea all along had been to alternate them in the roles of Hamlet and Horatio. The production was a big success. Putting too much faith in chance is a high-risk strategy, but not without success. Remember all successes have a quantum of luck somewhere, so do not ignore it.

The Director as Lovable Eccentric

This is the close relative of the director as believer in chance. The director is either genuinely eccentric or adopts that guise in an attempt to get extraordinary things out of the actors. The legendary Ken Campbell was the greatest of the genuine eccentrics. Beloved to the point of obsession by many actors, audiences, successive directors of The National Theatre and many non-theatregoers, Campbell hesitated at nothing.

OPPOSITE: Poster of *Man Friday* performed by 7:84 Theatre Company. In *Man Friday*, Adrian Mitchell reversed the roles of Robinson Crusoe and Man Friday, exposing the blind capitalist thinking of Crusoe and highlighting the wit of Man Friday. BART FIUT

Another director mentioned to the cast mid-rehearsal of a scene, 'I notice that nobody comes down to this corner of the stage. I'm putting some money down here, and it belongs to whichever character can, legitimately, come down here'. There was a rush to that corner!

The Director as Jolly Hippy

There is the kind of director who manages to treat the whole business as if it's the best joke in the world. Everything is easy, the whole cast are adorable, what can go wrong? The late Michael Bogdanov was a very successful director who was not only a jolly hippy, but met the world with a smile and a laugh, and directed some important productions, including Brenton's *The Romans in Britain*.

So what is the purpose of this semi-serious list of different shades of director? It is to indicate that there is no one way to direct a play. A versatile director needs to have bits of all of the above, and their own personality running through it all. One element that has become less apparent over the years is the idea that putting on a play is fun! Perhaps because the financial climate in which plays are produced now is colder, which in turn means directors earn less, which then means that a lot of younger directors are in evidence, who take it very seriously (as all directors do in the early stages of their careers). Actors, directors, designers – no-one in the theatre is well paid, so it should at least be enjoyable. If it's enjoyable for the performers, there's a good chance it will be enjoyable for the audience.

WHAT DOES A DIRECTOR ACTUALLY DO?

Interpretation

The director may or may not choose which play to do, but will certainly decide on the interpretation of the play. What do we mean by interpretation?

If the play is classical or from an earlier period, the director must decide what the context of the production will be. Will the actors wear Shakespearean doublet and hose, carry swords and wear wigs, or will it be in modern or contemporary dress? The considerations are financial, political and aesthetic. Financial, because it is clearly much less expensive to clothe the actors in modern dress than in full Elizabethan or eighteenth-century costumes. It is political in the sense that in doing the play you want it to have some relevance to the audience, and you must decide if that connection will be better made using one look rather than another. Will *The Merchant of Venice* mean more to a modern audience if it's set in the London Stock Exchange or if it is in period costume? The answer is not always obvious. An audience can get fed up of having modern 'relevance' pushed at them. If you decide on a modern look you must be careful how you deal with strictly period things, such as swords. It's not so much a problem with *Romeo and Juliet* where knives can be substituted for swords in a modern setting but what will be the solution with *Twelfth Night* in the scene with Andrew Aguecheek 'duelling' with Viola? There are several references specifically to swords. A recent production at The National Theatre, in modern dress, chose to simply ignore the anomaly, which was not satisfactory. Shakespeare's plays were, of course, performed in contemporary dress, so it could be argued that putting them in our contemporary dress is the right approach and in that tradition. However, the problem still exists.

The same questions apply to the setting. It is not just the designer exclusively who chooses the setting. The director says he wants to do a production of, say, *Love's Labour's Lost* and set it in it in colonial India – for whatever reason. The designer then takes that initial idea and develops it. Many plays today are performed on a single set, which is not location-specific but creates an atmosphere and is related to the emotional world of the play. The set for my own production of *Measure for Measure* reflected the emotional content of the play. I asked the designer to set it in a wrecked church – somewhere sacred that had gone to ruin, like Angelo, or like the state of Vienna. The image came from St Luke's church in central Liverpool. This church was bombed and caught fire in the Second World War and while the walls have remained, the rest of it was gutted. The whole interior is filled with growing trees with branches stretching out through the glassless windows. The set for the play had echoes of this 'bare ruined choirs, where late the sweet birds sang'.

Again, in my own production of Brecht's play *Schweyk in the Second World War*, I could not get a grip on the feel of the play. Walking in the fog along a beach with snow on the ground I had a clear view that this was like the last scene where Schweyk meets Hitler. From that recognition, the rest of the play fell into place – the square, forbidding walls for the Nazis, contrasting with the warmth of the pub and the necessity to build monstrous puppets for the figures of the Nazi high command, seemingly towering figures until the end when Hitler appears as a human-sized character in the snow.

For *She Stoops to Conquer* there is no question – the demands of the script make it very hard to modernize. In a modern dress production you would have to explain, for example, how the young men could have lost their way from London to Hampshire. What about sat nav? The play is about mistaken identity. What about identifying who people are from social media? It just doesn't work.

Again, the present writer directed Mozart's *The Magic Flute* and wanted to the production to have a modern feel, so went in for heavyweight directorial decisions about location and period. The first decision was to think of the Queen of Night as a reclusive rock star, similar to Madonna in her *Vogue* period, holed up in a penthouse suite in a skyscraper somewhere closely related to New York. All the other decisions about the production stemmed from that one idea – Papageno as a roadie, Sorastro as multi-media mogul converted to ecology and so on. The designer, David Collis, converted this starting point into an amazing series of settings and costumes.

So, by interpretation the director is bringing together the financial and time constraints with the imaginative look, feel and impact s/he wants to make with the production.

You will notice the plays instanced here are mainly old, period plays. Modern plays are nearly all set contemporaneously. The most difficult decisions about the period in which to set a play are usually plays that are recent, but neither entirely contemporary nor period pieces. So a play that was contemporary thirty years ago poses a real problem. Does it become a period piece or are the issues and the language of the play still current, and will it be better to set in the here and now?

The two great decisions a director has to make are the way the play is going to be interpreted and subsequently who is going to act in it (*see* Casting in Chapter 4). If you can get these two right, in combination with a good play, of course, then you are on the way to something positive – not guaranteed success, because that is an elusive thing. How to guarantee it is beyond human comprehension!

Bringing Clarity

The second role of the director is to bring all the diverse elements of the production together. There are two things to say straightaway about this.

First, it can be a cause of great frustration when it seems, at times, that no-one else understands the production. It seems incredible that people should ask questions that are important to them, but that to the director, betray the fact that they seem to know nothing about the production. The point here is that the director has lived with the ideas longer than anyone else, so ideas, concepts and casting decisions have become second nature, but might

have only just been communicated to the person who seems to be asking ignorant questions. They seem to be ignorant because they *are* ignorant! Ignorance is forgivable; it is stupidity that is harder to forgive. With the best internal communication system in place it is still possible – no it is likely – that you know more than anyone else about the production. Once again tolerance is required.

The second thing is that there is a lot of fuzzy thinking about the arts in general and the theatre in particular. As a hangover from nineteenth-century Romantic ideas about 'the artist', there is the very handy cliché of calling actors, or anyone else working in theatre, 'luvvies' or 'thesps'. Richard Wagner, among many others, promoted the idea that the artist was somehow above the hurly burly of everyday traffic. The artist was somehow in touch with a higher power, and this excused him from knowing about everyday things. This still persists. So there is a rough and ready assumption that a director will be hopeless at administration and public speaking because the director has profound artistic issues to deal with that elevate the director above day-to day-things like being on time, being civil or doing administration. It is a delusion that is often subscribed to by other people working around the director.

This is wrong. The great artists are good at many things. It is an error to think that talent is shared out equally. A fine actor might well be a good writer, painter or composer as well. Many such talents may be hard to acquire, but the one that is essential for a successful director is to get a basic knowledge, ability and enthusiasm for budgeting and doing straightforward administration.

In order to have proper, adequate control of a production, the director must learn and understand all aspects that relate to it – even those things that seem a long way removed but still impact on the production.

3
PRE-PRODUCTION – SELECTING THE PLAY

Like so many things – decorating and DIY, making a business presentation or speech, cooking a good meal or a party – preparation is crucial. The jokey advice I was given as a young director was, 'Stay a page ahead of the actors', and while that's always a good idea, the director needs to be rather more than a page ahead to comfortably lead the cast through the ups and downs of a rehearsal period.

GENERAL

Remember the Audience

Whichever way you come to directing, whether it is from a university degree course or from stage management or acting, the reality of putting on a play is more complex and intriguing than it probably seems from the outside. This chapter is a guide to getting started on a production once the money has been raised and a venue has been secured, omitting the touch of conceptual imagination that will make the production individually your own.

University graduates, in particular, will want to bring to bear the knowledge they have learnt about Artaud, Grotowski, Brook, Ostermeier, McBurney, Mamet and so on. Stage managers and actors will often come to directing because they have experienced first-hand good and not-so-good directors.

OPPOSITE: Benjamin Britten's chamber opera *The Rape of Lucretia* at the Dartington Festival. Note the sand giving a gladiatorial effect and the deeply emotional lighting (designed by David Collins). ARNIM FREISS

They perhaps feel inspired by the good, who have made it seem easy, and annoyed by the not so good, who have caused them hours of frustration – directing as an act of revenge!

The most important consideration is what the audience will take away. Who will your audience be? There is no more important conversation to have among the creative team than, 'Why are we doing this?', 'Who is this for?' and 'How will we attract them?'.

If you are running a theatre company you will want your choice of plays over a season to have some sort of continuity, maybe even a theme. On the other hand, a freelance director will be thinking, in the first instance, of plays that have a personal resonance and, secondly, where they might find a home.

In both cases the important thing is to think about the audience. Too often in the conversations directors have with actors, designers and others involved on the creative side, the dimension of

---

CONSIDERATIONS WHEN CHOOSING A PLAY TO DIRECT

- Does it really interest and excite you, the director? You have to enthuse others over a long period, so it needs to speak to you very directly.
- You should know what audience the theatre expects to attract.
- Can you cast it impressively?
- What kind of play is it?
- Does it cry out for a virtuoso lead actor, or is it more of an ensemble piece?

the audience is missing. There can be resentment when a marketing or administrative person talks to the director and says the proposed play is inappropriate because it won't find an audience. The tendency is for the director to want to choose a play that is adventurous, exotic or off the beaten track, whereas the administration generally wants to err on the side of caution. This caution is often reflected in the governing board of a theatre as well. So the director often has to be very well-equipped to make the case for the production. The director must assemble a collection of strengths about the play so that it is irresistible.

A Style to Attract a Loyal Audience

A glance at recent theatre history shows that those theatre buildings or companies that have a recognizable identity, are also those that generally do better at the box office. For example, Northern Broadsides, a company dedicated to playing the classics with a north of England accent or dialect, has had a great record of success both artistically and at the box office. The Theatre in the Round in Scarborough under Alan Ayckbourn likewise has – over the years – offered its audience plays with a mix of middle-class comedy and penetrating social observation with great success. The same can be said of the Glasgow Citizens in the 1980s when it specialized in decadent *fin de siècle* spectacular. The Royal Court in London has a mission to nurture new plays. Other theatres with a clear identity include The Arcola Theatre, with its preference for tough, contemporary work, and The Finborough and Orange Tree, all three in London, which have concentrated on reviving neglected classics of the twentieth century. So, in choosing plays for a building, an identity of some sort would be preferable to the generalist, something-for-everybody approach.

The theme linking a series of plays does not have to be explicit. It could just be an overriding idea that the director has in mind, which pushes the choice of plays in a particular direction – a taste for plays that reflect notions of justice, like the Tricycle Theatre in north London, or a preference for plays exploring local circumstances, like The Theatre Royal Stratford East.

So much for the general, more philosophical questions; let us now turn to the nuts and bolts of pre-production planning. So what kind of preparation should the director be making? Obviously choosing the play is the first thing.

CHOICE OF PLAY

A group of actors were at a dinner party with bankers and City people. After three-quarters of an hour the hostess made this observation, 'I've been overhearing all your conversations and so far all my friends from the City have been talking about plays and theatre, and all you actors have talked only about money!'; and, of course, that is the truth. In circumstances where money is scarce, it becomes the focus of interest. In preparing for a theatre production it is absolutely necessary to be realistic about the resources available. Sometimes

---

Eight Self-Improvement Strategies for a Director

A successful director has an instinct for the strange marriage of novelty and innovation with familiarity and reassurance. So where does that instinct come from? Some are born with it, others create it for themselves. How is it acquired?

- By knowing a broad spectrum of plays.
- By always reading old *and* new plays.
- By noticing how things go in cycles.
- By watching what the national trend-setting companies are doing.
- By talking with other theatre people about the kind of plays they like or know about.
- By going and seeing plays anywhere, and not being snobby about it. Great ideas can come from the most unlikely of places.
- By creating a reservoir of ideas and possibilities, the director improves the chances of choosing something that has legs.
- Read, watch, talk!

unrealistic assumptions are made about the box-office potential income. The intended play might be a favourite of the director who won't believe that the world might not share that enthusiasm, and be willing to turn out on a cold night, travel for nearly an hour and pay good money to see the play.

It also has to be a play that the director can fall in love with – even if only temporarily – because the director has to convince the other creatives and the cast to fall in love with it too. The director cannot proceed easily if there is anyone on the creative team or the cast who is militantly against the project. Everyone needs to be convinced. This is where the question of the personality of the director is of supreme importance. S/he must be able to sweep along everyone concerned, creating a feeling of confidence that the production will succeed.

Returning to the dinner party with the bankers, it is no good having fantasies about any project unless it is properly budgeted. From the outset you need to know the sort of costs involved. Obviously these will vary enormously depending on the play itself, and in what form it is going to be put on: whether a 'profit share' (so-called!); hiring a known venue; putting on a site-specific show; working in an established fringe venue, a regional theatre, or at an important London venue. (Let's assume that if it is in a prestigious venue, the director will almost certainly have gone beyond the limit of this book.) Whatever the idea, get a broad estimate of the costs before getting so carried away with the possibilities of the project that you can't let go of it, even when common sense tells you to get out. They say that theatre is very easy to get into, but very hard to get out of. You have been warned!

WHERE DO YOU SOURCE PLAYS?

The choice of play will depend largely on a combination of the taste and interest of the director, the location and the audience that the play is intended for. But where do you source plays?

Obviously there is a group of plays that the director will have seen, read or performed in, and very often plays experienced at an early age leave a great impression. A director might well want to revisit a play that was first encountered through school, university or youth theatre.

There are publications such as *The Guide* and *Catalogue of Musical Plays*, both published by French's, that give a very useful breakdown of the cast sizes and gender. Similarly, Nick Herne Books publishes *Plays to Perform* with a cast breakdown and plot synopsis of the plays licensed by them. StageAgents also publish a useful guide. *The Stage* newspaper lists current productions and reviews several plays each week and is a useful resource in getting to know the catalogue.

The internet is a very useful source. It is a good idea to look up the archives of theatre companies rather than trawl through the internet in a vague search. Look up the past productions of all shapes and sizes of companies, not just the obvious ones like the National Theatre or the Royal Shakespeare Company. Is there a company whose work particularly appeals? Then get to know its history of productions, through its website, where there is very often a list of past productions or perhaps through a book about the company or theatre building.

The career of a particular director or an individual actor is worth investigating to discover what plays they have been attracted to.

The adaptation of books and films into stage productions has often been a very fruitful source of an interesting project, and they come with a title, which can help to sell the play. From stage versions of Laurie Lee's book *Cider with Rosie* to the film *The Graduate*, there have been many great successes from these originals. Choose carefully – the great Cameron Mackintosh had a terrible failure with an adaptation of *Moby Dick*!

DIFFERENT TYPES OF PLAY

Plays are traditionally advertised along the lines of: 'Alan Ayckbourn's hilarious comedy', 'Arthur

Miller's searing family tragedy', 'Shakespeare's timeless tragedy', 'Stoppard's ingenious comedy', 'Faydeau's fast and furious farce' and so on. Within the broad definitions of comedy, tragedy and farce there are very many variations. What type of play a director is attracted to will depend on personal taste, the venue's policy, the availability of the rights, casting and costings. In approaching backers or venues, all these aspects need to be covered.

Serious and Tragic

A serious play or tragedy is easier to get right on stage than a comedy. It would be hard (but by no means impossible) to take a scene like the visit of Isabella to Claudio in *Measure for Measure*, when he is in prison, give it good atmospheric lighting, some music and let the words be clearly understood, for it not to achieve a reasonably acceptable level of emotional communication at the very least. However, with comedy the audience is either amused or not; there isn't a middle way. For comedy, the requirement is for actors who understand the nature of how comedy works. Not all directors or actors have that.

Modern and Period

The other big divide in types of plays is between modern/contemporary and period plays. There are currently fewer period plays being produced and more new or recent plays available. Obviously cost is a factor – size of cast, cost of period costume if used – but the difficulty schools have in teaching period plays and organizing theatre trips also contributes.

Theatre has also been used for social and political purposes. There are many directors and actors

OPPOSITE: The Cratchit Christmas dinner from Dickens' *A Christmas Carol* at the Haymarket Theatre, Basingstoke, adapted by Richard Williams. Many directors have written and adapted plays and novels for a particular cast or theatre company. ARNIM FRIESS

who want their work to do more than just entertain. Would you find it more satisfying if your work, directly or indirectly, contributed to current social debates?

Music

Musical theatre and opera will be covered elsewhere in this book, but the director should consider if music is an element that would enhance a production, and indeed if it is something that would make an interesting career option.

Physical Theatre

Physical theatre has become mainstream. Through the work of James Thiérée and other innovators in circus skills and non-verbal theatre, physical theatre has become a highly regarded part of theatre. Of course it reaches back in some ways to Commedia dell'Arte, but given a contemporary twist it can boast the humorous worlds of James Thiérée, the more serious atmosphere of Gecko and the hybrid world of speech and movement with Frantic Assembly.

THE ROBERT WILSON STORY

Robert Wilson, the now famous international stage and opera director, started out performing his own shows in shop doorways in Manhattan after the shops had closed. He couldn't get anyone to employ him so he started doing what he wanted to do where he could find a space and an audience. We know so much about successful people when they've become famous, but it is very enlightening to learn where they started out. Apart from the determination that story illustrates, it is worth a young director learning about the way people they admire in the theatre have made a career, and understand that there is an element of luck; an element of making your own luck; and an element of chance in the people you meet and work with.

Text-Based

Text-based plays can be divided into ensemble and non-ensemble plays. This is an important division because the approach and the atmosphere in the rehearsal room will be affected by it. I made a discovery when I directed *Hamlet* and had the resources to cast most of the parts separately, with a cast of sixteen actors. There are only four or five major roles, which means that there will be a large number of the cast who are in danger of becoming semi-detached from the production. The director needs to appreciate this before rehearsals start and think about the implications – by working hard to keep the (probably younger) actors in the supporting roles balanced with the more experienced actors in the principal roles; or the actors in the smaller roles could be cast in a companion piece like Stoppard's *Rosencrantz and Guildenstern are Dead*.

Ensemble

In an ensemble piece all the actors are used most of the time. For example, in a production of a classical Greek play the director could create a very actively involved chorus. With the resources for only a small number of actors, a production of *A Midsummer Night's Dream* could successfully double the roles of the Mechanicals and The Lovers with only minimal editing of the text.

One of the benefits of creating an ensemble is that there is a tendency to play to the strengths of each member of the group. This in turn creates a strong and sinewy production, as all the actors in the company get a chance to play heavyweight parts in different plays. This can yield a depth of casting that is sometimes hard to achieve when casting the plays individually, even at the higher levels of theatrical production. In addition, an ensemble of actors – permanent or semi-permanent – dictates the style and choice of production, because it only makes sense to use the whole group in each production. That way, a hallmark company style emerges.

POTENTIAL DIFFERENT AUDIENCES

Most young directors spend time and money thinking of directing a show in an established theatre venue. In thinking about choice of play, the director should consider all potential audiences.

Schools

There was a very strong movement called Theatre in Education (TIE) at the end of the last century and there is a large body of work that directors would do well to revisit. The topics divided between school issues – bullying, drugs, school and family relationships – and larger scale historical and social issues – the thalidomide tragedy (*The Apple of Our Eye*), the environment (*Drink the Mercury*), prison and capital punishment (*Example*). The generation of directors who emerged in the 1980s onwards often started out directing school shows in a TIE company. Touring a small-scale show to schools is tough, but will give invaluable experience, which is what a young director needs most.

Seniors

Another neglected area is theatre for the elderly community. Drawing on the local history as remembered by older people can be the basis for a very strong local drama, and the audience of older people will enjoy both contributing to it and seeing the finished result.

Space

The director should think about the space in which a production could take place. The idea of adapting the children's book *The Railway Children*, which was performed at The National Railway Museum, and played subsequently at London's

Waterloo and King's Cross stations, is a perfect example of lateral thinking. Look at a space and consider what might be possible to harmonize with the space. The National Theatre of Wales has also become celebrated for its productions in many different non-theatre locations.

Treat everywhere as a potential performance space. What could be performed in a restaurant, in a wood (apart from the many productions of *A Midsummer Night's Dream*), next to a memorial, in a museum or art gallery, in a car, a football pitch, on a train? There was a company called Tube Theatre, which advertised a meeting place on a tube platform, and then set off with the audience as passengers on the tube. The two performers performed a series of sketches, much to the amusement of the audience, who fooled other passengers thinking they were two real people.

Most plays are between ninety minutes and two and a half hours. But there is no prescribed length, so think about the shortest and longest possibilities. Some Samuel Beckett plays are only minutes long, and *After Liverpool* (James Saunders) is a

great collection of short scenes that can be performed anywhere.

GETTING PERMISSION TO PERFORM THE PLAY

Let us suppose that the director has chosen a play, which suits his/her taste. If it is a play by an author who died more than seventy years ago, there is no problem with rights.

The question of copyright must be taken very seriously and the director, or the appropriate person in the organization, must be sure that the correct rights are available for the type of production the director has in mind. The rights for plays with music are also very important to sort out well in advance. The penalty for not getting the correct clearance of the rights could be the legally enforceable closure of the production at any stage. Apart from the loss of money, no director would want to have that sort of scandal attached to his/her name.

The simplest way round the question of rights is to approach the literary agent who represents the author, or the estate of the author if deceased. The name of the agent will be in the front of the published copy of the play, or if unpublished, then a search on the internet will find the author's agent. If the play has not yet been published and other sources fail, then The Society of Authors or UK Theatre should be able to help. There is a very useful directory called *Contacts*, published by *The Spotlight*, which every director should have as a basic reference book.

Rights can be withheld if another company has taken out an option on the play. So, for example, in the past, the National Theatre paid money for a period of time to have 'an option' on Brecht's *The Threepenny Opera*. This meant that no other company could get the rights to perform it for that period. Plays with music will often have separate restrictions on the musical arrangements and sometimes specify the instruments that are to be used in the production.

WHAT ABOUT COPYRIGHT?

To quote the law specifically, a work is deemed to be out of copyright:

- Seventy years from the end of the calendar year in which the last remaining author, which includes a translator, of the work dies.
- If the author is unknown, copyright will last for seventy years from the end of the calendar year in which the work was created. If it is made available to the public during that time (by publication, authorized performance, broadcast, exhibition, etc.), then the duration will be seventy years from the end of the year that the work was first made available.
- Sound recordings: fifty years from the end of the calendar year in which the work was created, or if the work is released within that time, seventy years from the end of the calendar year in which it was first released or published.

Rights could be withheld if the work is being filmed or is being produced by another company. Plays do get simultaneous productions in different theatres, but the rights might be withheld if a Number One tour (a tour to large-scale theatres) or a West End production is being planned.

Sometimes there are specific restrictions attached to a play. So, for example, the choreography of *West Side Story* has to be the same as in the original production, and female productions of *Waiting for Godot* have been challenged in court by the Beckett estate.

The laws and regulations surrounding copyright are extremely complex. There are lawyers and law firms who specialize in it. It is beyond the scope of this book to go into the details, other than to say the director must be sure that all aspects of the necessary permissions are in place before starting on the preliminary stages of the production.

SCRIPTS

Having obtained the rights to perform the play, the production manager must get scripts for the cast, creative team, marketing, wardrobe and so on. In the case of a new play, the script will come from the agent and the company will photocopy it. If it is a published play or a translation of a foreign play, then it is important that the director is clear about which published version is being used. For example, there are numerous translations of Chekhov and Brecht plays. Plays written in English might have changes between different editions. Again the director must be clear about which version is going to be used before anyone buys a copy or sends copies out to the actors.

Scripts should be sent out to the actors as soon as the contracts have been signed. (It is not usually the job of the director to deal with contracts. That is the producer's job. It is advisable for the director not to get involved with negotiating actors' fees, as this could spill over into resentment if either side feel they have done badly from the negotiation.)

TRANSLATIONS

Translations tend to date very quickly. This is because in commissioning a translation, a director or producer intends to make the play more immediate to the contemporary audience. So the translator will often use words or phrases that are current at the time of writing the translation. Of course language is always changing and the more up-to-date the translation, the quicker it goes out of fashion. If at all possible, it is a good idea to commission a new translation, unless there has been a good one recently commissioned and for which the rights are available.

The other alternative is to get a translation that is no longer in copyright (*see* Box). Using this as a basis, the director or a writer can produce a new version of the play.

WORKING WITH AN AGENT

From this discussion it might seem that the director's or producer's interests are diametrically opposed to the writer's or composer's agent – this would be wrong. The agent wants to achieve two things. First, to get the writer's work produced but, second, to make sure the production is in the best interests of the writer. Hence the restrictions if there is an intention to film the play or a West End production is coming up.

The director needs to cultivate a friendly professional relationship with agents, whether representing writers or actors. By finding out which agents the director gets on with and with whom a good relationship flourishes, the director can begin a career-long relationship. The agent will suggest plays their clients have written or would like to write, and a good agent will understand the interests of the director and, where appropriate, make suggestions.

COMMISSIONING A PLAY

The director will often want to commission a play from a living writer. This can be very eye-catching

The Life and Opinions of Tristram Shandy commissioned by The Oxford Stage Company for a run in Oxford and a national tour. Laurence Sterne's highly unconventional, comic novel found a very sympathetic adaptor in Peter Buckman. In the photograph, Uncle Toby is reminded by his servant, Trim, how Tristram's nose was bent at birth by misuse of the forceps. ALISTAIR MUIR

as critics and audiences are often more interested in new plays than in revivals of classics. Working with a writer can be both rewarding and frustrating. Rewarding because everything about the play is new and affords opportunities for discovery, and because writers are – generally speaking – interesting people who can bring a new dynamic into the rehearsal room. Frustrating because the director sometimes has a particular idea in mind, which is not what the writer produces; or sometimes there are differences of opinion when it comes to editing the writer's work.

The two ways of going about commissioning are:

- To go to a writer with an idea for a play and, if the writer is interested, offer a commission.
- To find out what a writer is interested in writing about and offer a commission.

Writers are keen to have their work staged, so there is rarely a problem in getting a writer interested. The usual route would be to talk to the writer's agent and outline the project. If the writer

A scene from *Mind Your Head* by Adrian Mitchell commissioned by the Everyman Theatre. A surreal bus journey intertwined with the *Hamlet* story. Full of contemporary references, which is one of the great attractions of commissioning a new play.
CAROL BAUGH

expresses interest, then the director must meet and give details of the proposal. It is important for the director to be clear about the size of cast that is affordable, the kind of audience it is to play to, the restrictions of the theatre it will play in, the dates and deadlines and, in general terms, the overall anticipated feel of the piece – is it to be serious or comic, political, philosophical or musical? The writer needs to be suited to the commission. If the director is looking for an adaptation of a book, then a writer who has successfully done that before is probably the first port of call. Once the idea has been discussed, there should then follow subsequent meetings to flesh out the ideas the writer is suggesting and consider all the possible details. The deadline for delivery of the script must allow plenty of time for casting, designing and possible rewriting.

By establishing a relationship with literary agents a director can be introduced to writers and their work. Literary agents are, of course, keen to get their client's work produced and will send copies of plays for a director to read, and will be very interested in supplying information about the ongoing writing projects their client writers are engaged in. After the introductions, and if a particular idea strikes the director as something s/he is interested in, then a series of meetings will take place so the details of where, when and how can be discussed.

After a timescale and the size of the production, in terms of the cast and production values, have been agreed, the writer will go off and produce the draft of the play. This is an exciting moment for the director to see how an idea has been transformed into a reality. If the script is everything and more than the director expected, then the way is open for the process of scheduling it into a theatre's programme can begin. However, if the script is not what was expected, some carefully managed diplomacy is necessary. The most likely problems are:

- The length of the play – too long or too short.
- The cast size or cast requirements.
- The story is not what was imagined by the director.

With a generous writer none of these problems should be insuperable. However, the director must be diplomatic. It was the director who approached the writer in the first place because the writer had a record of producing what the director thought he wanted.

In the case of the length of the play, it is usually too long rather than too short. Shortness is not so much of a problem, but editing a play, which the writer has lived with for months, is sometimes difficult. The director must have specific ideas in mind for editing, backed by clear reasons. Simply saying the play seems too long is not enough. I worked with the poet and playwright Adrian Mitchell on several plays. He had a technique for dealing with suggested cuts from the director or actors. In response to the suggestion for a change on the script, he would say, 'Yes, let me think about that overnight'. The director or actor would be happy that their idea was being seriously considered. The next day Mitchell would come in and say, 'I've seriously thought about it and it should stay as it is'. In contrast, Tom Stoppard was very open for cuts, edits and changes.

The size of the cast or any other logistical problem will result either in the writer agreeing that something must change, or the director agreeing to find resources to meet the special requirements of the play.

If the outcome is not what the director had expected, then it is often the case that a director has lived with the general idea of the project over a period of time and has invented his or her own version, which is not what the writer has produced. In that case the director must get rid of the imaginary version and concentrate on the actual version. It is the *director* who should change rather than the writer. In an extreme case, if the director and writer cannot agree, the play might have to be postponed, cancelled or given to another director.

One lesson that comes through time and time again is that a great deal of what a director does depends on the director's disposition. As mentioned in the previous chapter, the director needs to be artistically imaginative and persuasive, clear and determined, but charming and engaging.

Having worked solo on the project to this point, the director next needs to engage with the creative team s/he has put together to work on the details of the production itself.

A scene from the opera *Rosenkavalier*, created for Joanna MacGregor's *Deloitte Ignite Festival* at the Royal Opera House. The world of the play is emphasized in this glittering, self-regarding, mirrored world. (Designed by Jane Janey.) TRICIA DE OURCY LING

4
PRE-PRODUCTION –
GETTING READY

MAKING A SCENE BREAKDOWN CHART

It's very useful for the director to write a Scene Breakdown Chart. The stage manager might well produce one for their own use when calling people for rehearsal, but it's an extremely good way for the director to get to know the play.

Having read the play a couple of times, the director needs a page or two of graph paper, or a program like Excel. Down the left-hand side, write the names of all the characters, and across the top, in columns, the acts and scenes or, if a modern play, the sections you have divided the play into. Each scene that the character is in should be marked with a tick or a cross. If a non-speaking character is in a scene, then the cross should be put in brackets. At the foot of each column, more information about the scene can be noted, for example the location and the main action of the scene.

Using the Breakdown Chart it is straightforward to see how the play is constructed, as far as the entrances and exits of the characters are concerned. In a classical play you can see what opportunities there are for doubling characters if, as is likely, you are doing a Shakespeare without an actor for every role. You will also find it easier to remember the construction of the play and the order of the action of the play.

By creating the Breakdown Chart the director will get a good idea of the way in which s/he will approach the play. The overall style of the production might still be uncertain but, at the very least,

it will possible to decide on the way the casting is to be organized.

The casting will be done either through personal contact or through the actors' agents. Having understood how many and what kind of actors are needed, in terms of gender and age, in the production, the director can move on to auditioning.

ACTORS' AGENTS

The director should subscribe to *The Spotlight*, which is the best directory for actors. Each entry will give the details of an actor's height, hair colour, recent parts played, singing range, instruments played, accents, and agent's name and contact details.

The usual routine for learning if an actor is free is to call the actor's agent. This is more reliable than actually asking the actor personally because actors are generally 'people pleasers' (a very good and generous quality) and this means they are quite likely to want to be positive and might give you the impression they are available, when there are other possible jobs in the wind.

As a subscriber to *The Spotlight* the director can look up the actors s/he wants to enquire about. The director should next draw up a list of the possible actors for each role. Then with all the details of the production at hand – performance dates, rehearsal dates, venues for performance and for rehearsal, names of director, designer, other actors so far recruited, the part for which the actor is being considered, the financial arrangements, anything else relevant – the director should ring the agent

	1.1	1.2	2.1	2.2	3.1	3.2	4.1	4.2	4.3	4.4	5.1	
EGEON	X										X	FATHER OF ANTIPHOLUS TWINS. ADOPTED DROMIO TWINS. WIFE = ABBESS.
DUKE	X										X	IS HE SEVERE OR COMPASSIONATE?
GAOLER	X											CAN DOUBLE AS OFFICER IN 4.1 + 4.4
FIRST MERCHANT		X									X	
ANTIPHOLUS OF SYRACUSE		X		X	X				X		X	BUSINESSMAN.
DROMIO OF SYRACUSE		X		X		X	X	X	X		X	CAST AS FEMALE.
ADRIANA			X	X				X	X	X	X	ANXIOUS. QUICK TEMPERED.
LUCIANA			X	X		X		X	X	X	X	CALMER. REASSURING.
DROMIO OF EPHESUS		X	X	X	X		X			X	X	CAST FEMALE.
ANTIPHOLUS OF EPHESUS					X		X			X	X	BUSINESSMAN.
ANGELO					X	X	X				X	SMART, WEALTHY MERCHANT.
BALTHASAR					X							NOT AS WEALTHY AS ANGELO.
LUCE					X							KITCHEN GIRL.
SECOND MERCHANT						X					X	NOT AS WEALTHY AS FIRST MERCHANT.
OFFICER						X				X		DOUBLES AS GAOLER.
COURTESAN									X	X	X	SEXY + FUNNY.
PINCH										X		WILD MEDICINE MAN. OR WOMAN.
CROWD										X	X	2/3 EXTRAS.
ABBESS											X	HAUGHTY BUT MELTS RECOGNIZING
	TOWN SQUARE	STREET	FRONT OF EPH HOUSE	STREET	STREET	STREET	2ND MERCHANT HOUSE	HOUSE OF ANT. EPH.	STREET	OUTSIDE BROTHEL	OUTSIDE CONVENT	

COMEDY OF ERRORS – BREAKDOWN.

OTHER COMMENTS.

Scene Breakdown Chart – a simple chart like this can easily illustrate the doubling possibilities and additional information about each scene can be added.
BART FIUT

and just ask. The director and the casting director will be calling agents very often so it's important to establish a good relationship. Agents like clear information from the director, and for all enquiries to be realistic. It would be unrealistic to ask Daniel Radcliffe to be in a stage production for no pay, but he might be interested in a suitable charity event. In other words use your common sense.

The agent will be able to say if the actor is available for the dates in question, and should also be able to suggest if it is the kind of production the actor in question would be interested in. If the actor is available, then the director can thank the agent and say s/he will be back in touch. If the actor is not free and the director does not have a good list of alternatives, then s/he should ask the agent if there are other possible actors on their books who are free. Over a day or two of being in touch with agents, a picture will begin to emerge of the possible casting.

CASTING

In considering what play to choose, the director should think of the casting opportunities and challenges. Is there a wonderful leading part that a named actor might be interested in? Is it an ensemble piece? How well known is the play and when was it last produced? Is the author's name a draw? Two out of three attractions or a high score on all are needed. The possible areas of attraction are:

- The play itself.
- The cast or company.
- The writer.

So, *Twelfth Night* (1, very popular play) at the National Theatre (2, very prestigious venue) with Tamsin Greig (2, well known, though not a household name) written by Shakespeare (3, the most performed writer in the world).

Looked like a guaranteed success – and it was!

However, it doesn't mean that everything by Shakespeare will attract an audience. There are about half a dozen of his thirty-seven plays that can usually draw a guaranteed audience – *Midsummer Night's Dream*, *Twelfth Night*, *Hamlet*, *As You Like It*, *Romeo and Juliet*, *Comedy of Errors* (perhaps) and *Julius Caesar*. Other people might choose a couple of different ones, but one attractive feature alone does not make a play irresistible.

It is a mistake to assume that a well-known actor will automatically bring in an audience. The name of the actor needs to 'fit' the production. An actor called Robin Askwith became famous through starring in a series of very light comedy films. When he appeared in Brecht's *The Resistible Rise of Arturo Ui*, a play about the rise of Hitler, the audience who liked Brecht couldn't imagine it with an actor known for that brand of film, and vice versa for Robin Askwith fans. In contrast, the Tamsin Greig example is a perfect combination.

Poor casting can be the death of a good project and, conversely, imaginative casting can turn a middling play into something worth seeing. Good casting rarely saves a poor play. So what is good casting? It's fulfilling the obvious demands of the play and mixing in surprising or adventurous choices. It pays to think laterally. Examples could include Rik Mayall in his *Young Ones* period, or as a frantic but resourceful Khlestakov in *The Government Inspector* at the National Theatre; David Threlfall, known for playing northern working-class characters, as *Hamlet*; Betty Marsden, a comedy actress from the radio show *Round the Horne*, as Asdak in *Caucasian Chalk Circle*; Meow Meow the cabaret artist as Titania at The Globe.

It is sometimes possible to suggest a piece of casting to an actor that the actor hadn't thought about but that completely suits them, at that point in their career. Charles Sturridge's production of Chekhov's *The Seagull* featured John Hurt as Trigorin. Given John Hurt's film commitments

---

A Lesson from the Glasgow Citizens

In the 1970s, a triumvirate of directors ran the Glasgow Citizens Theatre. Within two years it was the number one destination for actors. Everyone had heard of it and everyone wanted to work there. Why was that? What was the magic?

- The choice of plays was a bracing combination of new and 'classic plays' – like Shakespeare and Wycherley, and modern, like Brecht and Arthur Miller.
- The directors were not afraid to be controversial. They faced much opposition from local councillors but played to full houses.
- A style of play that was a winning combination of high camp, outrageous costume and high-definition acting.
- A young but extremely talented roster of actors, including Mark Rylance, Pierce Brosnan, Celia Imrie, Glenda Jackson and Lewis Collins.
- Encouraging the actors to take risks and be aware of the audience.
- The choice of plays and the chosen style of presenting them – plays with powerful themes, great parts for actors, and powerful and clear direction.

Airbase by Malcolm McKay at the Arts Theatre, London. Mark Rylance, Greta Scacchi with Kevin McNally behind. McKay taught at RADA, so he was in a good position to cast both Mark Rylance and Kevin McNally, ex-students of his, to star in the production of his own controversial play. ALISTAIR MUIR

it seemed unlikely he would have the time or the interest, but he was happy for the suggestion. The lesson here is that you should follow up every idea. You have no idea what a well-known actor wants to do next, and a new play, even at a small venue, might be just the right thing. Well-known actors are inundated with scripts and script ideas, most of which are copies of what made them well known in the first place. They are sometimes pleased to have something different to work on, if the timing with other commitments can be made to work.

WORKING WITH A CASTING DIRECTOR

Should a young director engage a casting director or cast friends from the local youth theatre, or college, or university, or from drama school? At the start of a director's career it is likely the cast will be actors known to the director. This is good for a director because it is very likely that at the beginning, the director will have to get used to several new circumstances both inside and outside

Robeson – Song of Freedom by Andy Rashleigh. The role of singer, actor and activist, Paul Robeson presented a casting challenge – find an actor who could sing like Paul Robeson. Leon Herbert was cast after an intensive auditioning process.
ALISTAIR MUIR

the rehearsal room. Familiar faces in the cast can make life easier as a young director finds his/her feet.

As the director gains experience and fewer unexpected issues arise, it is advisable to work with a wider choice of actors. A mixture of people who know you (and, importantly, respect your ambitions as a director) with some new faces is an ideal combination. Most directors accrue a loosely associated company of actors who they return to production after production. However satisfactory this may be, it is always important for the director

to expand the group of actors they are working with.

At the beginning of a director's career s/he should get to know actors directly by organizing and holding auditions themselves; but as they get established and busier, they should work in tandem with a casting director. It may be tempting to be surrounded by the support of a casting director, but the director needs to test their own instincts and see how their reactions in audition translate into the right casting choices in the rehearsal room and on stage. The director needs to create that

King Lear with Anthony Sher and Jonathan Pryce at the Everyman Theatre, Liverpool. Alan Dossor, the then artistic director, had an unparalleled talent for spotting raw talent. CAROL BAUGH

reservoir of known actors before handing over the responsibility to the casting director, because there should be dialogue with the casting director, not just a silent acceptance of their suggestions. There is no dialogue if the director does not know which actors are around.

AUDITIONS

The director and casting director draw up a list of people to audition. In putting together a timetable for the day, the time allocated to each actor will vary depending on the type of production and what stage of casting you have got to.

The accepted etiquette is that any actors who are well known, and especially if they are older, are not expected to present an audition speech. However, any actor will expect to be asked to read from the script of the play you are holding

auditions for. When talking to the actor's agent, the director should be very clear about what will happen at the audition. Will the director want an audition speech? Will you ask the actor to read from the play? Will there be another actor to read with the candidates? What is the part they are auditioning for? This all looks very obvious, but it's so much better to be careful, and avoid any embarrassing situations. It's almost inevitable that as you progress as a director you will have auditioned people who subsequently become well known. If you have an enticing project later in your career you will want everyone you ever auditioned to have had a civilized encounter with you.

The schedule should include some breaks, both to catch up and to have a coffee/loo break. Auditioning needs organizing. It is always advisable to have someone with you to ring an agent if someone doesn't turn up and, consequently, to rearrange the timetable and to deal with anything else.

A colleague will be a useful sounding board when you come to decision-making.

The audition room should be arranged with a table for yourself and your assistant director or stage manager, and a chair for the candidates. It needs to be well lit so both parties can see each other, and free from junk. Because rehearsal rooms can be expensive, it is tempting to crush in as many auditionees as possible, but this should be resisted. Actors must be treated with respect.

An audition is a serious undertaking for both parties. It will usually be conducted in a light and friendly manner, but both sides have to reveal something about themselves. Also, the well-being of the production might well hang on the way in which the director conducts the audition. The audition is almost certainly more of an ordeal for the actor than it is for the director, and it is important to be empathetic. The director should establish a friendly but formal relationship. The actor won't be impressed if you are drinking coffee, eating a sandwich, playing with your iPhone and so on. The background of each actor won't necessarily be clear from their CV, and so make no assumptions about them from the kind of work they have been doing. In a precarious profession actors very often find themselves doing all sorts of strange jobs. Just because they took a job as Father Christmas does not mean they are not a good actor. Everyone does something for money from time to time.

The auditionees' CVs should be arranged in order, with things like your notebook and pen to hand. Start on time and keep to the timetable. It is bad manners to keep an actor waiting half an hour, and might put off the actor you end up wanting to cast.

An audition. The audition is conventionally set in a large, light studio to give every actor his or her best chance. If successful at this one-to-one meeting, the actor will be recalled to meet the producer and read from the play. RICHARD WILLIAMS

AUDITIONING FOR A STRAIGHT PLAY

Assuming that you are auditioning for a straight play (a drama that is not a musical or a physically based play, but which communicates through the spoken word), each actor should be allocated 15 minutes. It is difficult to keep to the scheduled timetable if each audition is for a shorter time. It is also good practice not to appear to be hurrying people. Assuming you are seeing people for youngish characters, you might want to hear an audition speech, have them read an extract from the script and have a brief chat. The agent has been told that the audition speech should be about 2 minutes long and reading the extract from the play will be about 3 minutes; you will then want to comment on it and have the actor read it again. That might leave about 5 minutes or so to answer any questions about the production and to ask a few things about the actor's experience.

The director should have an assistant or another actor to read with the actor who is auditioning, because the director needs to listen and watch the auditionees.

With an older, more experienced actor, the director is more likely to have seen the actor's work, or see from the CV that s/he has done some work that is right for the part in mind.

If early in the audition it is apparent that the actor is not right for the part, it is imperative to avoid hurrying the actor out. In a business that is built on chance encounters and reputation, it is important to always use common sense and good manners. No one knows where the director or the actor might meet in ten years' time!

At the end of the audition let the actor know what happens next. Everyone understands that if the part is being offered, then there will be a conversation about money with the agent. If there is no contact, then it means that on this occasion there is no offer being made. If there is another round of auditions, give an idea of when they will take place.

AUDITIONING FOR MUSICALS/ MUSIC THEATRE

For the director, auditioning for a musical releases him/her from the sole responsibility of casting the show. The musical director and choreographer will make their decisions on qualities other than the acting ability of a performer. In this case the casting becomes very much a group process, but the final decision rests with the director.

Because the requirements for a musical are much more quantifiable – the actor either can or cannot hit a particular note, or do a particular dance step – the initial auditions are usually much quicker. The actor will expect to be tested on all three of the so-called 'triple threat' – dancing, singing and acting. The audition will usually be in that order, because any candidate who can't dance adequately can be sent away, and the same with the singing auditions. There will usually be a requirement to dance in a group, as instructed by the choreographer, and to sing two contrasting songs that demonstrate the performer's vocal range and capacity. For the spoken part of the audition it is almost certain that Shakespeare or other 'poetical' speeches will not be acceptable. Because the musical world is more cut and dried than straight acting, directors from the straight theatre are often surprised at the instant decisions that the musical director and choreographer can make. On the other hand, the candidates will realize more readily than straight actors why they are not eligible for a particular role (more details in Chapter 7).

After the first round of auditions, performers who are seen again at 'recalls' (or 'call backs') will expect to learn a song from the show or something very similar to the style of the show. As the singing and dance auditions reduce the number of candidates, the acting becomes increasingly important. The musical director and choreographer will want to recruit a chorus or ensemble that is a mixture of people who are either excellent singers and dancers, or who have strengths in both but excel in one more than the other.

AUDITIONING FOR OPERA

The opera audition often has a more formal feeling than acting or musical auditions. The singers will know exactly if they can sing a role technically. They will come more formally dressed. They will sing one or two pieces – usually something from the opera in question. They won't expect to do an acting audition; although if recalled they will not be surprised to be asked to do some sort of acting or improvisation based on the sung pieces they have brought in. In my experience singers are usually very open to acting; they tend to take the audition less personally because for them the technical, sung part is the key element (more details in Chapter 7).

The audition situation is highly artificial and can be terribly stressful for some actors. Even a very good actor with a strong CV and experience in the national theatre companies, film and television can quite commonly have had a long time out of work. These are the vicissitudes of the profession. Desperation can creep in, and that can bring with

it all sorts of odd and unpredictable behaviour. Every director has experienced an actor clearly overcompensating at audition. The director must be prepared and be entirely sympathetic at auditions. Never underestimate how stressful an audition can be for some actors. If they have had a run of bad luck and been out of work for a long

ANYONE CAN GO ANYWHERE – TAKE CARE!

The theatre, and indeed the arts in general, remains a profession where it is possible to move from one job to another without taking relevant exams or other qualifications. This is one of the great attractions. A director can continue acting, if that is where they came from, or can decide to write something and reasonably expect to get it performed, or can incline more towards producing. It is because of this that it is always prudent to treat other people in the profession with respect and good manners. The most unlikely people can become influential and the theatre world is small. Most older directors can testify to that!

UNDERSTANDING HOW DIFFICULT LIFE CAN BE FOR AN ACTOR

- The director needs to remember there are several psychological difficulties an actor has to learn to deal with: for example, the sense of rejection from not getting a part, the periods of unemployment, watching other actors getting recognition, and the poor pay in many circumstances.
- No one can really explain what makes the difference between a good and a not good actor. Unlike (say) a good plumber and an inadequate plumber.
- There are technical skills that can improve an actor's performance, but there is a long list of actors who never had formal training and who just stepped out on to the stage with the gifts they were born with.
- Other actors have trained assiduously for years and *still* don't produce convincing work on stage.
- An actor cannot do much to advance their career in-between jobs. They can read plays and go to skills' classes, but not much else. Acting – some would say – is about reacting and it's hard to react to oneself.
- An actor is unlikely to start learning Hamlet, or any other part, on the off chance they'll be cast in that role.
- The director must understand that the actor has to live with a lot of doubt and uncertainty. Everyone lives with uncertainty, but for the actor it's very near the surface.

For the director it's different. The director can usefully spend any downtime by reading, reading and reading. The director can also go and see productions and plan possible productions, which is very important – because the director goes out and sells ideas – for productions that, hopefully, will actually happen. No director should ever feel at a loss as to what to do between jobs.

time, their confidence can be very low and that can lead to some odd behaviour. In a rush to do a speech about a downhill skier, an auditionee jumped on the table the director was sitting at so the director was looking straight at a pair of knees. Another – as his confidence waned – drew nearer and nearer to the walls of the audition studio and ended up talking to the wall. The director must be sympathetic and remember what an artificial set-up the audition is. That said, most actors breeze in, do their stuff very well and cheerfully leave again.

At the same time as thinking about casting, the director will be working with the rest of the creative team.

THE PRODUCTION MANAGER

Probably the most important member of the team that the director recruits is the production manager. A good production manager will be reliable, flexible, financially literate, enthusiastic about the production and have a long, ready-made list of equally reliable contacts. Because it's a difficult job, many directors work with a limited number of production managers, relying on the expertise of someone they have come to trust over a number of productions.

The production manager's job is to convert the director's and designer's ideas into concrete reality. At the first meeting the director and designer(s) will outline their ideas about the production. While the production manager will want to know as many details as possible, a good production manager will know that some aspects of the play will develop both in the pre-production and the rehearsal periods. It is very important that the director develops an instinct for the realistic level of changes that can be made.

An absolutely critical decision for the production manager, together with the director and designer, is the budget. Everything will flow from this. At their first meeting the director and designer should explain the approach to the production in detail.

The production manager needs to know:

- The overall budget.
- The period in which the production is set.
- The number of performers in the cast.
- Who is playing what role and what doubling there will be (if any).
- Everything that might involve extra expense, such as additional stage crew to do a complicated scene change or costume changes.
- Details of the set and scene changes.
- Details of costumes and costume changes.
- Where rehearsals will take place. In some cases the production manager might have to organize this.
- What stage management have already been recruited.
- All the significant dates of the production.
- Who is responsible for the lighting design.
- Who is the composer and what instruments are required (if any).
- Who is the wardrobe supervisor in charge of the costumes.
- Contact details for everyone involved.
- Any special considerations, for example children involved in the show.

Having understood as much about the production as the director and designer, the production manager takes away the model of the set and the costume drawings, to cost the production.

The budget must be as exhaustive as possible. Here is a list of the pre-production (everything up to the beginning of the first performance) budget headings as a guide:

- Director (one-off fee for rehearsals, up to and including the technical rehearsal, dress rehearsal and first performance).
- Designer (one-off fee for rehearsals up to and including the technical rehearsal, dress rehearsal and first performance).
- Everyone else on the creative team:
  o Actors/singers (how many, rate of pay, number of weeks).

o Stage management (ditto).

o Musicians (ditto).

o Lighting designer (one-off fee for pre-technical rehearsal rigging and focusing, and then up to, and including, the first performance).

o Sound designer (ditto).

o Fight director (one-off fee for rehearsals and technical, dress and up to, and including, first performance).

- Set (everything the designer has included – floor covering, flats, ceiling piece).
- Furniture (all the furniture that will be required).
- Costume (for all actors, including any changes of costume).
- Wigs (less used these days, but very expensive and not to be added at the last moment).
- Props (again everything that is almost certain to be used. However, props are an area where it is likely there will be changes and additions in the rehearsal room. Include hires, such as weapons).
- Additional props and furniture (some allowance for the material added in rehearsal).
- Special requirements (something that doesn't fall into any of the above categories).
- Lighting (very often only gels for colouring, but sometimes hiring special lighting effects, e.g. rain effect, or for buying specific gobos).
- Computer-generated images/video (increasingly used in productions).
- Sound.
- Special effects (smoke and haze machines, dry ice, explosions, fireworks).
- Rehearsal room hire (self-explanatory).
- Scripts/scores (bought, hired or photocopied).
- Rehearsal props (a small amount for stand-in props in the rehearsal).
- Transport (moving the set from the workshop to the theatre; cost of the stage-management team collecting props).
- Refreshments (tea, coffee and biscuits in the rehearsal room).
- Marketing (if you are working in a conventional theatre set-up it is likely that there will be an annual marketing budget, which covers each production; likely to be budgeted by the producer not the director).

If you are producing in a less conventional set-up – say a site-specific event in which you are the producer as well as the director – then you must take into consideration a long list of other costs: getting power to the site, security, parking for the audience, insurance and so on.

The running costs (all the costs incurred while the production is in performance) include:

- Actors.
- Stage management.
- Musicians.
- Hire of performance space.
- Running props (anything that gets used and needs replacing during the run, e.g. foodstuff and drinks, cigarettes, furniture, crockery, etc. that gets deliberately broken in the performance, and so on).
- Stage effects (e.g. replacement smoke canisters).
- Lighting and sound (unlikely to need running budget, but think about it).
- Costume (maintenance of costume and replacement if the production demands it).

Post-production (things that need paying for after the last performance) budget items include:

- Transport (for disposal of the set and returning hired/borrowed props).
- Storage (if the intention is to revive the production).
- Contingency (in addition to the above, you need to add 10 per cent of the total to deal with unexpected additions and emergency events).

Income budget headings include:

- Anticipated sales at each seat price range, including differences for matinees and Saturday evenings.
- Merchandise – anticipated sales of programmes, badges, CDs, etc.

BUDGET
NAME OF SHOW
DATES OF REHEARSAL
PLACE OF REHEARSAL
VENUE OF PERFORMANCES
DATE OF FIRST PERFORMANCE
DATE OF LAST PERFORMANCE

PRE-PRODUCTION

Fees

Director	£
Designer	£
LX Designer	£
Sound Designer	£
Production Manager	£
Musical Director	£
Vocal Coach	£
Choreographer	£
Fight Director	£
Video Designer	£
Other	£

Actors

Number of actors	at £	per week = £
Number of actors	at £	per week = £
Number of actors	at £	per week = £
Number of actors	at £	per week = £
Number of actors	at £	per week = £

Musicians

Number of Musicians	at £	per week = £

Stage Management

Stage Manager for	weeks at £	per week = £
Deputy Stage Manager for	weeks at £	per week = £
Assistant Stage Manager for	weeks at £	per week = £
Assistant Stage Manager for	weeks at £	per week = £

Builds

Set Construction	£
Costume Construction	£
Wigs	£

Props	£
Furniture	£
Other	£

Hires

Hire of Lighting equipment	£
High of Video equipment	£
Hire of Sound equipment	£
Hire of Furniture	£
Hire of scores (musical and opera)	£
Hire of rehearsal room	£
Other hires	£

Other outgoings

Scripts	£
Transport set and costumes to venue	£
Rehearsal room refreshment (teas etc)	£

RUNNING COSTS

Actors

Number of actors	at £	per week = £
Number of actors	at £	per week = £
Number of actors	at £	per week = £
Number of actors	at £	per week = £
Number of actors	at £	per week = £

Musicians

Number of Musicians	at £	per week = £

Stage Management

Stage Manager for	weeks at £	per week = £
Deputy Stage Manager for	weeks at £	per week = £
Assistant Stage Manager for	weeks at £	per week = £
Assistant Stage Manager for	weeks at £	per week = £

Hire of space	£
Running Props	£
Stage FX (Effects)	£
Costume maintenance	£

POST PRODUCTION

Transport for return hires	£
Storage	£
Contigency @ 10%	£
GRAND TOTAL EXPENDITURE	£

INCOME

Value of house per week at 100%	£
Value of house Monday	£
Value of house Tuesday	£
Value of house Wednesday	£
Value of house Thursday	£
Value of house matinees	£
Value of house Fridays	£
Value of house Saturdays	£
Total	£

Box office		
Anticipated income	% of total =	£
Sponsorship		£
Trusts and Foundations		£
Arts Council/other funding bodies		£
Other		£
GRAND TOTAL INCOME		£
ANITICPATED SURPLUS/DEFICIT		£

OPPOSITE PAGE AND LEFT: Sample of a full-budget template for a production. Every show must be carefully costed from the start to avoid overspending or an over-estimated box office income. The director must be aware of all financial aspects of the production. BART FIUT

Depending on the agreement with the venue, there might be costs for front-of-house services.

It is essential that every possible aspect of the production is itemized and budgeted for. The last thing the director needs to be bothered about is an unexpected item that has not been budgeted.

Although even small companies now usually have a producer whose job it is to look after the money side of things, there are still many instances when the director is also the producer.

The production manager will call another meeting once the costing of the show has been completed. Present at this meeting should be: the director; the designer; the lighting and sound designers; the costume supervisor; the stage manager; and person responsible for props, if there is a designated individual. At this point it's very often the case that adjustments will have to be made to some of the production concepts. The set might be too expensive, the actors' bill too high and the rehearsal room hire too exorbitant, so changes will have to be made. The director and designer (with foresight) will have prepared for the reduction in costs and be able to offer creative solutions. *Flexibility is a primary requirement for a director.* The skill is to develop a middle-ground approach, somewhere between foot-stamping insistence on an artistic vision, as displayed in movies of the 1950s, and an inclusiveness, which dilutes the production ideas to homeopathic invisibility. This is the case not just for production meetings, but also for the overall day-to-day business of directing.

Having made suggestions about how to match the budget and the production, the production manager will repeat his costing exercise, call another meeting and hopefully by the third or fourth meeting (!) everyone will be satisfied. Once everything has been agreed, the production manager will be in charge of making sure that everything is ready to go on to the stage for the technical rehearsal, or earlier if a particular large or unusual prop needs to be in the rehearsal room, such as puppets, weapons and/or musical instruments.

The director, stage manager and production manager will need to meet to arrange the rehearsal schedule. This will not include the details of the scene rehearsals, which will change day to day in the rehearsal period.

There may be pre-full rehearsal calls for fights or music. If the rehearsal time is limited, then a few specialist calls in advance of the beginning of the full cast rehearsals are advisable. It can be a great boost to the production if, on the first day, some of the cast can sing their songs or some part of the fight sequence can be shown. More importantly it saves time in the full cast rehearsal period. Actors will need to be paid additionally for these rehearsals. Pre-rehearsing self-contained sections releases a lot of regular rehearsal time.

RESEARCH

A vital part of the director's work before the rehearsals begin is to research the play, the writer, the period of the writer's life, the period in which the play is set, the period in which the director wants to set his or her production, the costumes, music of the period – in fact everything!

Research can come from libraries, the internet, books, films, teachers, interviews, museums, art galleries and visits to locations mentioned in the play. For some directors research is almost the major ingredient in producing a play. For other directors research might be quite sketchy. The director does not want to be caught out in rehearsal not knowing basic information, but must be careful not to bore the rehearsal room with the new knowledge they have just gained from research.

The general schedule for the full rehearsals needs to account for warm-ups, fight rehearsals, dance rehearsals, costume fittings, photo calls for publicity – and anything else that can be predicted. Even if the actual time and day is not yet known for (say) a publicity shoot, it can at least be reasonably guessed at, so that the director can have it in mind as the day-to-day rehearsals are scheduled.

SHAKESPEARE

It Is Different!

Shakespeare is the most performed author worldwide, and it is inevitable – unless the director resolutely turns his/her back on it – that directing a Shakespeare play will be an expected challenge to the director. Shakespeare deserves special mention because there are particular considerations when directing a Shakespeare play, or other work from the late sixteenth/early seventeenth century.

First of all there is the language. It has to be admitted that, with differences in vocabulary, syntax and grammar, the text seems to have been written in a semi-foreign language. This doesn't produce insurmountable difficulty, but it is as well to acknowledge at the outset that for some actors, and directors, the initial reading of the play can be hard. It is useful to remember that if the final product is good, nobody is much interested in how it was rehearsed. Do not be afraid to start with very simple steps. You are going to direct your first Shakespeare play. What to do?

Understanding the Plot

The first step is to understand the plot! Many contemporary plays tell the story of one set of characters only, many with small casts. Most of the plays of Shakespeare and his contemporaries have intertwining subplots, and at least a dozen characters.

A bald synopsis can be a difficult read, so start researching by looking at a reputable film version, or a children's version, or anything else, that gives a simple start. It is not necessary to tell anyone that the research started by looking at a *Shakespeare for Dummies* (actually it's very good)! After watching or reading, the bare bones of the main narrative and the relationships of the main characters should be clear. Move on to reading a reliable synopsis, and draw a family tree of the characters. Try describing the story to a friend. Now read the play for the first time. Read it through quite quickly the first time, and don't get hung up on understanding everything. Look at the reliable synopsis again to check on the action of the play and the character relationships. Now read the play again *but slowly*, and take time to 'translate' unfamiliar words and curiously constructed sentences. Use parallel texts (available for free online) – Shakespeare plays in the original language put alongside a translation into modern English. Hopefully – by now – the play is feeling less of a mass of strange and difficult words and constructions, and emerging as a strong story with complex characters.

Once the play is familiar – that is, the story and how the characters relate to each other are completely clear – get a reputable, academically sound edition of the play. This will be a single play edition with only one play, not the complete works. The Arden, Cambridge and Oxford editions will all give you a good introduction to the play with details of the history, sources and all the main points of debate that scholars have discussed. What is required next is a delicate interplay between the research the director undertakes, and the director's own ideas.

What Period?

One of the most important decisions is to decide what period to set it in. There is an idea that – somewhere – there is an authentic production, which would look and sound just like the first production at The Globe Theatre in the early 1600s. However, critical changes have taken place since

---

THE IAMBIC PENTAMETER EXPLAINED

Shakespeare and his contemporaries wrote most of their plays in blank verse. Although the majority of actors know about the iambic pentameter, it is not a bad idea to remind the cast of the basics, which are:

- The iamb is one of the many different stress systems used in poetry.
- Its particular stress is de-*dum*, where 'de' is an unstressed syllable and *dum* is stressed.
- Pent is Latin for five.
- The iambic pentameter, therefore, has five iamb units. A perfect iambic pentameter has ten syllables, alternating unstressed and stressed. For example:
- 'If music be the food of love, play on.'
- The unstressed syllables are: if, sic, the, of, play.
- The stressed syllables are: mu, be, food, love, on.

The iambic pentameter can give the director and actor many ideas about how to deliver a line. The purpose of studying the rhythm of the writing should be to help deliver an understanding of the lines. It is not something to get hung up on. Indeed many actors will have studied Shakespeare so long that it is second nature for them to understand the underlying metre of blank verse without stopping to analyse it.

Research: look at John Barton's book and/ or video titled *Playing Shakespeare*.

---

that time. The changes are not so much in what is amusing, or in a person's feelings of love or anger, but in the fact that we know something about Freud and Darwin. We do not know what was in the mind of the audience at the first performance. Shakespeare's audience passed bear- and dog-baiting pits, cock fighting, brothels and the heads of traitors on London Bridge. There is simply no sense in thinking we can see anything through any but our own, modern eyes. A production dressed in the costume of the early seventeenth century can be very beguiling: very clear, very entertaining, very moving. But so can a production in contemporary dress.

Richard III at the Everyman Theatre, Liverpool. Clarity of speaking the text is the top priority in Shakespeare. Many of the plays vary from 'wide-screen' epic, with a large number of actors in a scene, to intimate 'close-up' scenes. CAROL BAUGH

Shakespeare's theatre used contemporary dress most of the time, with period additions where necessary, such as Roman swords and shields. The decision in which period to set the production is very often a financial one. It is usually less expensive to use modern dress and, for audiences, it often feels more immediate.

The World of the Play

There was a fashion in the 1980s to set classical plays in costumes from a mixture of periods. The intention was to emphasize the universal nature

of the plays – 'they don't just belong to a single period, but to all times'. This needs careful judgement from the director and designer in order to avoid the collision of styles just looking like a car crash. Done well, it can be arresting, witty and thought-provoking.

Suppose that for financial reasons the director is inclining towards a modern dress production; the important decision is to set the play in a period that captures the circumstances of the original. So *Julius Caesar* has often been set in fascist Italy of the 1930s. The National Theatre's production of *Richard III*, similarly, was very successfully set in an imaginary London under a contemporary fascist king. Kenneth Branagh's film of *Love's Labour's Lost* was set in the early twentieth century, and his *Hamlet* was early nineteenth century. More recently, the visits to this country of productions by The Toneelgroep Amsterdam of the Roman history plays and Thomas Ostermeier's *Richard III* have, respectively, set the plays in a contemporary newsroom and an expressionist no-man's land.

Whatever thoughts the director has about period, it *must* create some sort of recognizable world. Thomas Ostermeier's *Hamlet* was an expressionist extravaganza, but it created the world of Claudius' court as a drunken haven by having the cast sit at a table at the back of the stage drinking cans of lager. Brecht's production of his own play *Mann ist Mann* invented a world of monstrous, giant soldiers teetering on stilts.

Editing and Updating

Speed of delivery apart, there are some good reasons to examine the text carefully and, if helpful, to do some edits. Some references are now difficult to understand. Despite the early twenty-first-century fashion among many directors for not cutting any part of the text, where words simply do not exist in modern English there is every reason for editing or replacing a word with another that scans properly. Who now knows the word 'facinerious' meaning 'villainous'? Even a word whose meaning is quite possible to deduce – like 'maculate' meaning 'impure' – can take a moment to register. Some unfamiliar words are easy to understand in context: 'How will this fadge?' asks Viola in *Twelfth Night*, and we can immediately know by the context she means 'How will this turn out?'. Judicious editing and word-changing is entirely justified because the director's job is to let the play communicate. However, the director has a heavy responsibility to the author as well, so any changes should be discreet.

The Elizabethan audience was alert to words and not so much distracted by the visual, as our contemporary life is. Sometimes the complexity of construction of a passage makes immediate understanding very difficult; it would seem quite justified to make some edits to let the sense communicate much more readily. For example, the opening to *Measure for Measure* is hard for us to work out at one hearing:

> Of government the properties to unfold,
> Would seem in me to affect speech and discourse;
> Since I am put to know that your own science
> Exceeds, in that, the lists of all advice
> My strength can give you: then no more remains,
> But that to your sufficiency as your Worth is able,
> And let them work.

The director should assume the role of an audience member hearing the play for the first time, and should make the speeches comprehensible at a single hearing, but not simplistic. Once again, discretion and judgement must be exercised; without them the way is open for mayhem.

Doubling

It is almost certain that, outside the National Theatre and the RSC, Shakespeare productions will involve some actors doubling and taking more than one of the smaller roles. Some of these doublings have a long (if unproven) history. Shakespeare is alleged to have played Hamlet's Ghost. A case has been made for Cordelia and The Fool doubling in *King Lear*. The contemporary director may well want to reduce the cast size by merging two parts. For example, the same actor very often plays Fabian and Feste, and Fabian's words and actions are taken by Feste in *Twelfth Night*. The same can occur with Lennox and Ross in *Macbeth*. In these cases, two roles are made into one, which can help to reduce the size of the cast; but opportunity for this kind of amalgamation is quite rare. Much more common is the doubling of roles.

When doubling, it is important to try and minimize the shock for the audience. The best example is a very common doubling in *A Midsummer Night's Dream*: Theseus and Hippolyta with Oberon and Titania. This works well because the situations of the couples are similar. In the case of

Theseus and Hippolyta they are about to get married, but as Theseus says to Hippolyta:

Hippolyta, I woo'd thee with my sword
And won thy love doing thee injuries;

Oberon and Titania are fully engaged in argument, and Theseus and Hippolyta have been embattled, but the end of the play will reconcile both couples. Any doubling should – wherever possible – try to follow a few simple rules.

- Do not get the same actor to double two roles that are close to each other in stage time. An actor exiting as one character and immediately re-entering in a different hat as another is intrinsically funny, and almost certainly not the effect that is wanted.
- An actor changing sides or allegiances is unsatisfactory. So, if an actor in *Julius Caesar* were playing one of the minor conspirators, it would be odd for him to change sides and appear later as Lepidus.
- It is better if the actor who doubles is not memorable in some way – exceptionally tall or short – which will make the transformation into the second character less convincing.
- The further away (in the action of the play) the doubling occurs, the better. So Hamlet's Ghost could double with The Gravedigger, or The Player King with Osric, as they are all well separated.

Obviously, some adaptations make positive use of doubling. The Chapel Lane Company's version of *Romeo and Juliet* employed the idea of four public school boys performing the play, with successful results.

Fights

It is a feature of most of Shakespeare's play that there are fights. Mainly they are sword fights, and done well they continue the story of the play while adding tremendous excitement to the production.

It is very important that the director engages a reputable fight director; this means a person who has trained in stage combat, is qualified and holds certificates in stage combat. If something goes wrong, the director does not want to be held responsible for entrusting a fight to an unqualified person – this can lead to legal proceedings, so the director must make sure the fight director has got recognized qualifications.

The next consideration is the amount of rehearsal time the fights will need. The director – in consultation with the fight director – must allow adequate time for rehearsal. It is advisable to start on day one, and schedule a fight call on a very regular basis. This is an area where no risks can be taken. However, the payoff in terms of enhancing the production is great. A wonderfully choreographed sword fight at the end of *Hamlet*, or a battle in any of the history plays, is exciting and energizing.

If the director has decided to put the play in a modern setting, then the question of how to treat the fights must be seriously addressed. Actors in Armani suits suddenly getting involved with a sword fight could be inconsistent. Of course it is possible to synthesize the two in a setting that is expressionist or universal in its concept, but in a conventional transposition of periods, the questions of weapons and communication are the two stumbling blocks – why not use a gun and a mobile phone? Baz Luhrmann's film of *Romeo and Juliet* answered the question of weapons by using Shakespeare's words as the brand name of guns – so Mercutio's gun, seen in close-up, is a brand Dagger 9mm. This is not possible onstage. There are suitable answers to these questions, and mobiles and guns have been very successfully used in modernized versions of Shakespeare plays; but it is topic that must be approached carefully if the action is to remain plausible within a world.

With the pre-rehearsal work done, the director can confidently anticipate the next major step in the production process – the read-through of the play with the cast, and the excitement of weeks of rehearsal.

5

WORKING WITH ACTORS AND THE CREATIVE TEAM

ACTORS

Training and Background

Today the training of actors is increasingly diverse. In the past an actor would train at a drama school like RADA, Guildhall or Central, and his or her peers who were interested in drama but wanted an academic qualification went to a university. Today the dividing lines are blurred. Actors training at drama schools get degrees and students on performing arts' courses at universities can be on a course that offers a substantial amount of practical training. This is only relevant to the director in so far as s/he needs to understand that actors will have learnt many different approaches to creating a character and rehearsing a play. Actors from a drama school might have had a training focused on Stanislavski, Meisner rehearsal techniques or the ideas of Michael Chekhov, Ute Hagen or Jacques Lecoq. Others in the rehearsal room might have come from university where there has been a lot of opportunity to perform; actors might have learnt by experience onstage with student or professional directors, rather than from drama school acting classes. Another group might have come straight into the profession from another job, or from amateur theatre, or from school. Yet another group, older actors, might have come from a background where training was more like a finishing school.

OPPOSITE: Act two of *Carmen*. Carmen and friends sing and dance at Lillas Pastia's inn. This production took place in the cattle-auction ring, Kirkwall, The Orkneys, as part of the St Magnus Festival. JANE JANEY DESIGN

It is quite likely the director does not know all (or even any) of the techniques taught at drama schools and s/he does not need to know them. To know of them can be beneficial, but it is not a necessity. Given there is no single direct route through training that is common to the whole cast, the director needs to be careful about how s/he addresses the actors in rehearsals and not make any assumptions. To start using exercises or improvisations peculiar to one discipline risks leaving other actors, who don't know them, out in the cold. This is not to say the director should avoid any useful rehearsal techniques, but everyone involved must be very clear about how exercise or improvisation is set up, and the purpose and hoped for outcome. The director must also be certain that s/he knows exactly how to run the exercise. The director risks wasting time and losing the confidence of the cast by running half-baked exercises. In rehearsals for a production of *Around the World in Eighty Days*, an assistant director lost the trust of the cast by instigating a series of difficult and unresolved exercises, resulting in a vote of no confidence and him being side-lined.

Respect for Actors

There are a number of things that will help relations with actors.

TIMETABLE

Devise a timetable and stick to it. Some directors start the day with a warm-up. Some like to go straight into the scene rehearsals. Another approach is to start with all-day sessions at a table, exchanging research and working through the text in the manner of Adrian Noble. Others do a mixture of approaches, with an hour of table work analysing the text, followed by an hour of work on an individual character, followed by an hour of research (watching an associated film perhaps), and so on for the first third of the rehearsal period. Again, others will follow the more conventional approach. However you prefer to rehearse, do work out a timetable. Actors resent hanging around when they have been called at a certain time.

An overall timetable is best worked out by working backwards from the first night. This tells the director when the dress rehearsals will be, which will then: fix the technical rehearsal; fix the run throughs in the rehearsal room; fix the first stagger through; fix the time by which the individual acts need to be rehearsed. There will always be flexibility, but give the actors and creative team an overall plan. Importantly, let the actors know about any days off. Will there be rehearsals on any Saturdays? How will the director respond to requests for time away by an actor wanting to go for an audition elsewhere? What time of day will rehearsals generally end? The director might well say s/he is happy to give people time off with a day's notice, but not in the last week in the rehearsal room or in the production week.

DEADLINE TO BE 'OFF THE BOOK'

Be very clear by what date the actors should have learnt their lines. Richard Digby Day (a director credited with discovering Imelda Staunton, Ralph Fiennes and Hugh Grant, among others) would refuse to direct scenes with actors who had not learnt their lines by a pre-announced deadline.

NO PROMISES

However tempting, do not make promises that cannot be fulfilled. Even if someone else is responsible, it will look like the director's fault if things go wrong. In directing *Hamlet*, the present writer was led to believe by an important producer that the production would be going on an overseas' tour

after the initial run. When this fell through, the actors, obviously, were all contracted and the dates had to be filled by whatever was available. Birmingham did not seem as attractive as an ancient amphitheatre in Crete!

EXPLAIN THE APPROACH

Explain the approach that is going to be adopted in rehearsing the play: 'We'll spend three days researching and exploring the world of the play' or 'We'll spend a week translating *The Tempest* into modern English and then improvise the main scenes for the next two days' or 'I like to rehearse in a conventional way – we start at the beginning and work through scene by scene and then repeat, each time with more detail'.

BE CLEAR

Be very aware that money matters are important to actors, and dealing with money must be straight, even if the news is not good.

ELBOW ROOM

A final word: do be careful not to make the whole enterprise look too militarily precise or over-organized. The cast has got to feel there is room for their contributions and that the director will be happy to use and develop them.

THE REHEARSAL ROOM

The Room Itself

The rehearsal room should be the best the producer or director can afford. It is always worth spending the most possible on the rehearsal room, because this is where the work will be done; and a positive rehearsing environment will get the production off to a good start. One director found a disused fire station and negotiated to use it as a rehearsal space. It was a good size and as the production was happening in the summer, heating was not a problem. What was a problem was the state of the space. It was very dusty with a lot of litter. Nothing unpleasant, but it looked bad. The director thought it would be a good idea for the cast to have ownership of the space and the production by clearing out and cleaning the fire station the first two days. Unsurprisingly it had the opposite to the intended effect. If the space had been cleaned beforehand the cast would have been intrigued by its novelty, and it would have been a bonus. A light, heated, ventilated, tidy room will serve the purpose. It needs basic furniture to stand in for the set and furniture.

The Atmosphere in the Rehearsal Room

The feeling of the rehearsal environment is perhaps one of the most basic, but most difficult to define. The director sets the tone. Because acting talent is not distributed according to background or class,

the terms of reference, the general knowledge and the life experiences of a cast of actors can be extremely varied. It is, therefore, very likely that some very basic questions might come up in rehearsals. The director must create an atmosphere where anyone can ask questions without embarrassment. It is important to focus all the time on the production, and never use the rehearsal to show off directing skills or knowledge. Self-deprecating humour can be a very good way of creating an easy atmosphere, as can the confession, when an actor asks a question to which the director does not know the answer, 'I don't know, either, let's work it out'. The thing I learnt most from Richard Eyre was how to talk as the director during the rehearsals.

While humour is important, it is equally important to judge when to stop being light-hearted and let the actors know that you are taking the performance seriously.

The rehearsal room for Gorky's *Summerfolk* at the Drama Centre, London. A good-sized studio with the room laid out with the dinner table, with actual, or replacement furniture and props. RICHARD WILLIAMS

Discipline

It is important to create an atmosphere in the room where actors can feel relaxed, free to experiment and play. Counter-intuitively, the ability to play needs an uninterrupted and focused room. It is a good idea to establish a simple rule: any of the cast can come into the rehearsal to watch a scene, but they are either totally in the room or not in. To be totally in the room means watching and adding to the creative energy in the room. People must not be in the room reading a magazine, newspaper or fiddling with an iPhone. Make it clear that it is perfectly alright if cast members do not want to watch other scenes. Nobody will be thought of in a negative way if they do not come into scenes other than their own.

This is why it is important to have an additional room for socializing and line bashing. If it is not possible to arrange for another, adjacent room, then the director must stick very carefully to the rehearsal call, so that actors for a following scene do not interrupt a scene rehearsal in progress.

THE WORLD OF THE PLAY

The Basics for the Actor

One sure way to engage the confidence of the cast is to provide a clear description of the world of the play and the characters in that world. This is the product of the vision of the director combined with the work of the designer – unless the director's style is to explore and create the production from scratch with the cast. However, assuming the director and the creative team have decided on the world of the play, here are some examples offered as a guide. These production ideas were offered to the cast at the beginning of the rehearsals and helped to show the cast they were in safe hands, because the vision was specific and easy to reference.

Examples of Text-Based Shows

The Comedy of Errors Set in the mythical, sleepy Wild West town of a thousand cowboy movies. The Duke becomes Sheriff, and the gallows are set at the back of the stage throughout the action as a reminder of the darker side of the play. Country and Western music.

Hamlet Set in a court full of overheard conversations and scenes spied upon. The set is three enormous, black, silk drapes hanging from the flies down to the floor and across the floor to the front of the stage. Much whispering and billowing of drapes, as unseen characters listen in to scenes. Costumes an exaggerated eighteenth-century look. Movement like birds: some birds of prey (Claudius), others in flocks (The Court).

A Midsummer Night's Dream Set in no specific period but with emphasis on the 'night' and 'dream'. Costumes for all but the Mechanicals based on nightgowns, dressing gowns and pyjamas. Mechanicals 1950s. Bottom the Rotary Club bore, Quince earnest school master. The wood a series of shiny, metal ladders flown in from floor to flies, close enough for actors to cross the stage at a high level using the ladders.

The Importance of Being Earnest and *Travesties* These two related plays performed in repertoire. The nineteenth-century interiors of *The Importance* covered with dustsheets for the comic, memory play, *Travesties*. The colourful detailed set and slightly formal, more monochrome costumes for *The Importance* contrasted with white dustsheets and bright costumes for *Travesties*.

Magic Flute Set in a mythical New York/Gotham City. Queen of the Night a reclusive rock star, Papageno a roadie, Tamino a journalist looking for a scoop. Action moves from the Queen's hotel suite to several different floors of Sorastro's skyscraper.

Devised Script

In the case of a devised show, where the cast does not have the reassurance of a tried and tested script to inspire confidence, it is even more important to lay out the territory clearly at the first meeting.

A devised show on a social theme – the problems of Altzeimer's, say – should start with the director giving the cast assurance by having evidence of the starting point for research by the cast in the room. On day one, photos on the walls, piles of newspapers, film from the internet, books, addresses for contacts with home carers, onset Alzheimer's sufferers and doctors will all promote the engagement of the cast. The devised project must feel like a well-controlled adventure for the cast and not a vague, well-intentioned, but ultimately worthy and dull project. The opportunities for vibrant dramatization must be evident from the start to excite the performers.

DIRECTORS WITH ACTORS AND THE SCRIPT

Occasionally, directors will dispense with the script so they can concentrate on what the actors are doing in rehearsal. The Welsh director Peter Gill works this way. Most directors sit at a table in rehearsal (best to sit at one end of the stage manager's table; not behind the table, but facing the room with one elbow on the table with the script on it). However, the script can become a safety net for the director and the actor can get impatient if s/he thinks the director is not looking at the acting.

There is a famous story about Peter Hall directing Dustin Hoffman in *The Merchant of Venice* in London. Hall used to sit in rehearsal with his script on a music stand. He often smoked a cigar in rehearsal (this was before the smoking ban, of course), following the script intently. He was most anxious, above all else, that the actors rigorously followed the iambic pentameter and the sense of the lines. Hoffman had grown impatient of this behaviour and as he started the famous speech beginning 'Hath not a Jew eyes?', he undid his trouser belt and, without pausing in the speech, took down his trousers and 'mooned', then got dressed again to coincide with the end of the speech. Hall, who had not looked up during the speech, merely told him to observe a pause midway through a particular line. Cue suppressed laughter from the cast!

Do make the cast feel assured they are being looked at.

WARM-UP AND EXERCISES

Older Actors

One of the differences between more experienced actors and recent leavers from drama school is that the younger actors will be keen on warm-ups, physical and vocal, and keen on talking generally about the play. Older, more experienced actors, in general, are less interested in warm-ups; they want to get on with rehearsing the play and not talk about it so much. They might even be suspicious of research or other round-the-table work or improvisation. There is a famous anecdote about John Gielgud in a Peter Brook production of *Oedipus Rex*. As part of an improvised exercise, Brook asked each actor to come to the front of the stage and say out loud something that frightened them. When it came to Gielgud's turn he came to front of the stage and cried, 'We open the show in two weeks!'.

When asked about his warm-up for *King Lear*, a very famous actor said, that was what the first scene of the play was for. The older, more experienced actor can rely more on a deeply ingrained technique. The director must be careful not to push older actors into taking warm-ups. The older actor will be well aware that there are very many fewer parts for that age group, and will instinctively want to try and please the director. However, there are instances where over-exertion in a warm-up has had bad results with injuries to older actors.

Younger Actors

However, younger actors may not be up for everything. Actors in general are gregarious; they will say they like to take risks, that their actor heroes are the ones who seem to live life fully onstage and like to try anything. The director should realize that the risk-taking actor is quite a rarity. (By risk-taking we do not mean physical risks, but a willingness to risk acute embarrassment through improvisation or by revealing their private person in public.) In theory, every actor would like to play Hamlet. It is a career-making part, a star role that keeps the actor in the spotlight for hours in every performance; so, in theory, every actor would be desperate to play it. In reality, it is not clear that every actor would actually like to take on that responsibility. If *Hamlet* goes badly, then the actor playing Hamlet must take a lot of the blame. In theory, many actors would like to play Hamlet, but in practice would prefer to play Horatio, a part that puts the actor close to the protagonist but relieves the actor of the weight of the whole production being on his shoulders. In the best productions, the director has cast the play with a whole cast of actors who would fearlessly grab the centre stage and take full responsibility for the production. An ensemble like the Toneelgroep Amsterdam is formed of exactly that kind of actor. In the absence of a long-established ensemble in the UK, there is a scarcity of that kind of strong casting in every part.

THE DESIGNER

For the director, the relationship with the designer is central. If you look at the creative teams in any theatre you will notice that the same directors and designers tend to work with each other time after time. For example, director Katie Mitchell has worked with designer Vicki Mortimer over a period of more than thirty years; they began when they were both students at Oxford. The same is the case with lighting designers. This is because the visual aspect of a production reinforces and

The realized costumes and masks of the Gods from the drawing opposite. TRICIA DE COURCY LING

makes manifest so much of the director's vision of the production.

Together, the director and designer will complement each other's ideas and complete the vision for the production. Most directors have a general idea of what the production will be like, but the idea will not necessarily be fully formed. In a roundabout and discursive series of conversations, the two will come to an understanding of what will serve the production, and what is possible within the time and budgetary limits.

In a long-lasting and truly creative relationship, the designer may offer the director the springboard for the production. At other times, the director might have more formed ideas, which the designer will

Designer's sketch of the characters of the Gods from the *Good Soul of Szechuan* – what the director can expect from the designer. Sketches from the design team, Jane Janey, for the production of Brecht's play at The Platform Theatre, London.
TRICIA DE COURCY LING

Der Rosenkavalier *Richard Strauss*

ACT I. Vienna, 1740s. As morning sunlight streams into her boudoir, the Marschallin

Rosenkavalier Room- Walls lined with mirrors reflecting endlessly into each other, rococo dressing table with triple mirror and stool covered with scent bottles and regular sprays of perfume, candelabra, wig on a wig block, three dresses on dress stands, shoes, fans and hundreds of silver roses.

Performers have masquerade masks on sticks, swords, clutch bags etc.

Melancholic, slightly comic, unnerving

Sound extracts from opera, but highly distorted and played backwards, snippets about aging and identity/Shakespeare to Oscar Wilde/ adverts about anti-aging products/ conversation about ID cards.

A mood board – rough ideas from the designer to spark off a conversation with the director. This mood board for *Rosenkavalier* turned into the Mirrored Room, page 50. JANE JANEY DESIGN

finesse. Typically, the director will describe a mood or general feeling about a play. For a D.H. Lawrence play the director might start with: 'It should be very naturalistic. I'm thinking of the kitchen with a working tap and a real meal being prepared on stage in the action.' For a production of *Much Ado About Nothing*, 'I was wondering if it is too much of a cliché to set it at the end of the First World War, or do you think it should be more modern?'; or for a production of an Alan Ayckbourn play, 'I don't think it can work in any way other than strictly following what's indicated in the script, but we could update it as far as the costumes and props are concerned'. For a production of *The Jungle Book*, 'I wondered about starting with a young Kipling in his bedroom with jungle-patterned wallpaper that comes "alive" and turns into the jungle'; or again, 'What about doing *Dido and Aeneas* in modern

dress straight from Vogue?'. These opening comments will always be followed by, 'What do you think?'. There then follows what should be a very constructive, if meandering, conversation as different possibilities are explored.

So the director offers a starting point that the designer might follow; or it might be the catalyst for the designer to suggest something different, sparked off by the initial idea. But it is an exchange of ideas between equals.

Whatever the outcome of the first discussion, the designer will start to turn the ideas into detailed reality. First of all a mood board or suggested source material from magazines; later, sketches of the set and costumes; and, finally, when everything has been agreed between the director and the designer, technical drawings of the set and costumes from which the production manager

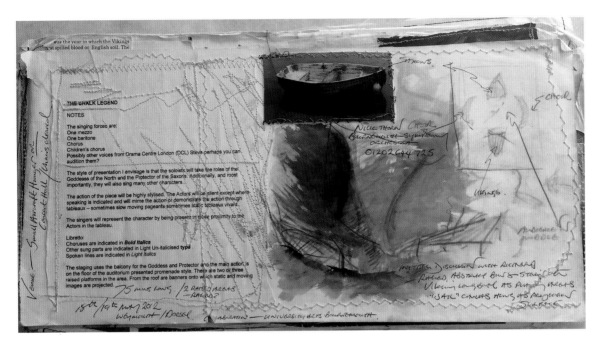

Another mood board using bits of the script as a basis. One of a series for *The Chalk Legend*. JANE JANEY DESIGN

can cost the production, and from which the set builder and costume maker can work.

Where does a director find a designer? One very good source is to look at the final degree shows of theatre design courses. The standards of the well-known courses are at a professional level. Among the best known are the theatre design courses at Wimbledon College of Art, The Royal Welsh College of Speech and Drama, Central Saint Martins and Nottingham Trent University. One obvious way

is to approach a designer whose work you have seen in production. In this case it would be sensible to match the resources for the production and the experience of the director with that of the designer. It's unlikely, though not impossible, for a high-profile designer (Vivienne Westwood, say) to want to come and design a show at a fringe venue for a novice director. It all depends on how exciting the project is, how persuasive the director can be and what new opportunities it offers.

THE KEY ATTRIBUTES OF THE DIRECTOR–DESIGNER RELATIONSHIP

- They will be constantly inspired and excited by each other's ideas.
- They can trust each other to fulfil the ideas/ vision of the other.
- They appreciate the work pattern of each other.
- They trust each other to complete their work in the given budgets and time-frame.
- They share common interests and reference points.
- The essential quality is trust.

THE LIGHTING DESIGNER

Everything above about the designer holds true for the lighting designer.

COMPOSER

It is less common to use a composer, although without a doubt the relationship of director and composer can be extremely creative. Songs or music as a soundtrack or a soundscape, are increasingly part of the expectations of a stage production. Specially commissioned music can work in very many different ways in the theatre. Music can give a conventional revival of a Shakespeare play an interesting modernizing twist or reinforce the period feel of the play. Music can mark endings and beginnings, and can also underscore important moments. Music supplies emotion not narrative. However, outside the national companies or with brand new, often student-created groups, the costs and time requirements make specifically composed music prohibitive. The emergence of the actor-musician is a welcome help for directors who don't have lavish financial resources. As well as adding a dimension of their own instrument to the production, it is often the case that good musicians can compose or improvise effective music too.

As with designers, composers can provide the initial idea for a production. Because their background is markedly different from most directors and actors, a composer's input can be a very welcome change. Classically trained composers will have a very extensive knowledge of the classical repertoire, and jazz musicians or singers will often be able to suggest ways in which actors with only a minimal musical ability can improvise effectively.

MUSICAL DIRECTOR/ CHOREOGRAPHER

When directing a musical or a music theatre production, a musical director will be necessary. Unless the director decides to specialize in musicals, s/he probably won't have the same close relationship with a musical director as with a designer; however, the role is crucial. Unless you are a musician as well as a director, you need an expert to get the musical content of the show rehearsed to an acceptably high level. Because of the ease of listening to music via CDs and the internet, audiences have a very high expectation of musicals

Costume drawings for the characters from *The Good Soul of Szechuan*. JANE JANEY DESIGN

THE ESSENTIAL MUSICAL REPERTOIRE

Over a period of time, a director should become familiar with all genres of music. This is an outline guide, a starting point only.

Gregorian chant	Faure	Categories of popular music of the twentieth century include:
Palestrina	Gershwin	
Thomas Tallis	Stravinsky	
Monteverdi	Copland	
Bach	Bartók	Blues
Vivaldi	Charles Ives	Disco
Handel	John Cage	Country and Western
Mozart	Steve Reich	Hip Hop
Beethoven	Philip Glass	Jazz
Chopin	Thomas Ades	New Age
Berlioz	The Beatles	Rock and Roll
Verdi	The Doors	Progressive Rock
Mahler	Frank Zappa	Punk Rock
		World Music

wherever they are performed. In small and medium productions the musical director will play the piano in rehearsals as the cast learn the music. In larger, more expensive productions there will be a pianist (called the repetiteur), as well as the musical director. As well as being responsible for getting the highest standard of singing from the cast and playing from the musicians, the musical director will also protect the singers' voices by reminding the director and choreographer that certain places onstage or positions in a dance can badly hamper a singer.

The choreographer will have a direct influence on the staging of a show. A musical, or a show with a lot of choreographed movement or dance, needs to be worked out in some detail before the rehearsals. For example, the director and choreographer need to agree on the direction of entrances and exits associated with a dance number. Because a musical is less 'naturalistic', it is generally easy to agree in advance the outline of the shape of a scene or number.

THE WRITER

The director has a relationship with the writer, whether the writer is living or dead. Much of the relationship with a writer of classical drama was referred to in the section on Shakespeare in Chapter 3. It is useful perhaps to be reminded that in working on a classical play there is the possibility of overloading the actor with background information. There is the historical period in which the play was written (e.g. Shakespeare's *Julius Caesar* 1599); there is the historical period in which the play is set (Julius Caesar's assassination 44BC); and there is today, when the play will be performed. The director needs to be circumspect about how much information the actor can usefully assimilate. The actor's job is to convincingly pretend to be a part of that story. Some background information will be helpful, but exactly how much, will be a critical judgement by the director.

A writer like George Bernard Shaw brings into the picture the detailed knowledge of his letters, written comments, broadcasts and his whole recorded life to add to the possible areas for research and discussion by the cast and director; but it will not guarantee a brilliant production of *St Joan.*

A director's relationship with a living writer can be one of the most dynamic aspects of a career as a stage director. There is a particular excitement about directing a world premiere. The writer–director relationship can have come about from an association at youth theatre, college, drama school, university or just by chance. The director must realize that while everyone in the theatre is anxious – actors, designers and directors, all aware of the scarcity of work and opportunities – it is worse for writers. For the others there are several different work opportunities, which might not be what they trained and hoped for, but at least the advert, the presentation skills' class, the understudying, the book design, the teaching, pays money and keeps them roughly in the right creative area. The writer lacks alternatives and will have a particular style or kind of writing, such as comic but not political, which limits the possibilities further. This means that the director must be very careful about raising false expectations. Sitting down with a writer and being encouraging about a play can be misinterpreted as a promise of a production, especially if the conversation drifts into fantasy casting. In the cold light of day the director admits that is a good, but not a great, play and the relationship with the writer risks becoming derailed – maybe permanently.

One of the complaints that writers have, and quite justifiably so, is that critics, audiences and actors frequently talk about the play not as written, but as *they* would have written it, if they had had the idea. In talking to a writer it is important that while ideas are explored at the series of meetings that must take place between a writer and director, the director helps the writer to keep to the parameters of the agreed draft, but not inhibit any novel directions the writer is taking. The writer will absorb ideas and frequently present a quirky, more interesting outcome from the conversation.

The director and the writer must be agreement about some aspects of the play. Often this is a successful partnership. Famous double acts have been John Dexter and Arnold Wesker, Peter Wood and Tom Stoppard, Peter Hall and Harold Pinter, and Richard Eyre and David Hare.

There is a tendency now for plays to be workshopped before progressing to being staged. A low-key rehearsed reading – a group of actors with the director and writer gently reading the play and talking privately about it afterwards – can be a milestone in preparing a play for production. However, held at the wrong time it can seriously compromise the authority of the writer by insensitive comments from producers, dramaturge, actors and anyone else present. The workshop for possible supporters should be left until the play has been carefully considered, and both the director and writer are sure the play is ready for a semi-public outing.

THE SOUND DESIGNER

Just as it is important to speak some of the same language as the designer, it is clear that a similar relationship should be established with all members of the creative team. In the same way as a director needs to have a knowledge of the history of theatre, a rough idea of the different ways actors train and a rudimentary idea of the main movements in art history, so it is with regard to sound. The director needs to be acquainted with the basic categories of musical development. As most people are in touch with pop music, but not so much with the classical repertoire, the rough list in the Box is a starting point. There are so many options, so it only scratches the surface. It is a starting point if the director is new to the world of classical music.

With good preparation from all the team working together, the director should be ready to go into rehearsals.

6
REHEARSALS – GETTING STARTED

WHAT DO YOU DO TO MAKE REHEARSALS WORK?

Some General Thoughts

A stage director is like a manager of a football team. The techniques for getting the best out of their cast or team are varied and mysterious, but it all comes down to inspiring confidence. Confidence in the director can come from the director's track record. Having had a series of well-received productions, or having worked with high-profile actors at a well-known venue, can all contribute to a feeling of confidence in the director in the rehearsal room. But what if the director is more of a novice without a striking portfolio of work to create confidence? Here it is more to do with personal chemistry or charisma. Both of these qualities are vague, but we know it when we see it, and recognize when it's absent.

By and large, directors and actors do not get paid enough to have a miserable time. The usual low wages must be compensated by:

- Doing something highly creative.
- Being creative in a positive atmosphere.

It is the director's function to make the rehearsal room a place of free speech, humanity, enjoyment

and creativity, and to do all this with a sense of moving forward.

There is no one method for running rehearsals. Every director picks up ideas from rehearsals they have been involved with if they're an actor; from their experiences as a student director putting together shows at college or university; and from tutors and directors if they've trained as an actor or director.

It is likely that the older and more experienced a director becomes, the less interventionist s/he becomes. As the director becomes more confident, the casting of a play becomes more accomplished, the director's methods become known and the actors arrive with some expectations. Hopefully, with some successes notched up, the director knows more clearly what will work and what won't. At the beginning of a career the director will probably work out, in advance, the close detail of all the moves, will have extensive research on the background of the play ready to pass on to the cast and will want to demonstrate to the cast that s/he has done their job, which probably

---

SOME BEHAVIOURS TO THINK ABOUT AS A NEW DIRECTOR

- Energetic but not manic.
- Good humoured but not idiotic.
- Generous but not a pushover.
- Clear but not simplistic.
- Direct but not rude.
- Well informed but not clever-clever.
- Organized but not obsessional.
- Artistic but not obscure.

OPPOSITE: Jade Ogugua as Mrs Shin from the production of *Good Soul of Szechuan* at The Platform Theatre, London. TRICIA DE COURCY LING

means talking more than they will later on in their career. Peter Brook describes it well in his important book, *The Empty Space*, when he talks about the detailed preparations he made for one of his first professional productions. He describes cutting out little figures for each of the characters and moving them round a model of the set. Once in the rehearsal room he realizes the limited value of this exercise when, as he describes it, he discovers the actors are so much bigger than he anticipated and they have a mind of their own.

You Just Have to Smile

It is very important that the director is confident about the production, and whatever this involves by way of preparation is entirely legitimate. It is important to remember that a theatre production is an exercise in optimism. Someone, usually the director, has had an idea for a play, or a theme for a devised play, and in the preparatory meetings that idea becomes refined and money starts to be spent. However, the whole thing is written in the air. Unlike other activities, like being in the property market or selling cars, where past experience can be a guide to the future, there is no guarantee of success in the arts. Just because something similar has been successful in the past it does not mean that it will be a hit. All experienced directors have known the surprise and frustration of a past success failing to repeat that success in a revival. The casting, the performance space, the ticket prices, the time of year, the *Zeitgeist* could all contribute to a previous success performing poorly at the box office the second time around. Very often a success is repeated, but it's far from guaranteed. So every time a new production starts, it is only kept afloat by the goodwill of everyone concerned. This usually makes a rehearsal room a place of great positivity. This is one of the great attractions of being a director or an actor. The working environment is usually constructive and positive. On the other hand, this positive, optimistic attitude can mean that a director and cast keep committed

to a production when every indication is that it has reached the end of its natural life.

A GENERAL NOTE ON REHEARSALS

At the start of a new production, the director must communicate faith in the project to everyone in the room. It really doesn't matter what has been involved in the preparing for the production. What follows is a description of all the stages that might be involved in rehearsing a play. It is the approach that would be taken in a non-experimental, conventional situation.

Before the first day of rehearsal, the director and the designer have met and agreed set and costumes (as described previously in Chapter 4), and will not anticipate much to alter in the rehearsal process. By the time of the first read through, some of the costumes may already have been started. Almost certainly, the building of the set will have commenced. The stage manager or the props manager might have ordered some of the major props. This is mentioned in order to draw attention to the fact that, in some ways, the conventional approach to theatrical production is rather inflexible. In this model of putting a production on stage, the costumes and set do not emerge organically from the discoveries and decisions in the rehearsal room. On the other hand, it can be reassuring for the actors to know what they will be working with from the very start of the rehearsals. They will know that the wigs and boots have been budgeted for and so start to imagine wearing them. They can look at a model of the set and realize how many steps there are to get to the upper level, and so on. From the point of view of the director, this points to the necessity for exquisitely detailed planning in the pre-production period, and very close work with all other members of the creative team. If, at the start of rehearsals, the composer can play some of the music that will underscore a key passage, if the fight director can show where on the set the fights will take place, if the lighting designer can give an idea of the mood to be created in some parts of the action, then the actors can begin to feel confident that they are in an environment where they can trust the director. It is critical that the director does not promise or suggest things that are unlikely to happen.

However, there will always have to be an understanding between the actors, the director, the designer and the wardrobe department that during the rehearsals there might be changes. So wiggle-room is essential, but mainly for practical purposes. Many decisions will have been made in advance, but the director should present them sensitively, with a sense that there will be exploration and discoveries to be made about the play in rehearsal.

A NOTE ON STANISLAVSKI

Stanislavski is the great inspiration for all modern stage (and screen) performance. As such, the director should know about his system and the principles he enunciated. He suggests the actor and director should ask a number of questions about

A VERY BRIEF GUIDE TO STANISLAVSKI'S SYSTEM

Stanislavski evolved a system to help actors achieve great naturalism on stage. He listed seven basic questions for the actor to consider in relation to his character:

- Who am I?
- When am I?
- Where am I?
- What do I want?
- Why do I want it?
- How will I achieve it?
- What will prevent me from achieving it?

He added thoughts about physical relaxation and circles of engagement.

His system was extended and formalized in the USA by Lee Strasberg who, in particular, concentrated on emotional recall.

the character and consider the circumstances surrounding the appearance of the character in a scene.

While it is important for the director to know about the system, it is not the only way to achieve a good production. Indeed many actors have achieved great performances while being totally ignorant of the system, while many actors have made it so much part of their unconscious thinking about performance that they would be shocked to be asked to use it consciously.

The way in which a director can use it valuably is as an occasional reminder to an actor. So the director might ask, if s/he thought it would help progress the scene, 'And perhaps remember exactly what it is you want to achieve in this exchange with the other character' or 'I think you could be stronger in playing what you see as the obstacles in this scene'. A light touch will do. If the actor wants to talk about 'given circumstances' and 'who I am', then the director will join in that conversation.

THE FIRST MEETING AND READ THROUGH

Getting started is always a difficult moment. The usual, straightforward starting point is a meeting with the whole cast, the producer, the stage management, the other members of the creative team, the company's administration team, or at least the marketing people and senior administrative person, the wardrobe – in fact as many interested parties as possible. It is important to get everyone together so that there can be a proper sense of a united purpose.

The aim of this meeting is to introduce everyone concerned to each other and to read though the play. Although this is the conventional start to rehearsals, it is very important to bear in mind that for the actors this is a very testing moment. The director has cast the actors; they have read the play and had some ideas about how their character journeys through the play. But now, in front

[handwritten top: diagram with x marks, "about", "xxx"]

PART ONE THE CREATION

[handwritten: God in organ loft]

<u>Scene 1 - The Creation and The Fall of Lucifer</u>

[GOD IN THE PULPIT. CAST SING OR HUM WITH PERCUSSION UNDER GOD'S OPENING SPEECH.]

[handwritten: SOUND FX ____ LX/GOD ?]

GOD   Ergo sum alpha et omega
                Vita, via, veritas
                Primus et novissimus.

[handwritten left margin: vita, veritas, vovitas]
[handwritten: Doth it need translation]

                I am gracious and great, God without beginning.
                I am maker unmade, and endless shall be.
                I am life and the way unto wealth winning.
                At once with my blessing I bid that here be
                A bliss all shielding about me. SOUND FX
                In the which bliss I bid there be here
                Nine orders of angels full clear ① SOUND FX *
                In love everlasting to praise me. (ANGELS HUM)

[handwritten right margin: Hit the alliteration; LX ANGELS. (5)]

[CAST ENTER AS THE ANGELS] — *[handwritten: enter under me; LX ADS (7)]*

                Here underneath me now a place be riven — *[handwritten: Hate]*
                Which place shall be Earth. It shall be as I say,
                Earth/② SOUND FX

[handwritten right margin: LX EARTH. W.DGN.]

[AN ACTOR RUNS THE LENGTH OF THE CHURCH WITH A GLOBE SPINNING OFF CLOUDS ACCOMPANIED BY MUSIC]

             and now Hell; *[handwritten: LX 5 Hen. (0).]*

[A <u>PYRO</u> GOES OFF WITH TIMPANI ROLL] SOUND FX

             this highest be heaven   *[handwritten: LX.6(0)]*

[APPROPRIATE HEAVENLY MUSIC !]

                Joy shall attend all those who here stay.
                This I give you ministers mine
                The while you are stable in thought
                But I warn that those who are not,
                Shall be put in my prison in pain. ③

[handwritten right margin: Joy in the thought; LX 7 Hen.]

                Of all the powers I have made, most next after me, *[handwritten: LX 8.]*
                I make thee,

[handwritten left margin: diagram with G, x marks]

                [INDICATES LUCIFER] ④ — *[handwritten: come forward]*

                As master and mirror of my might;   *[handwritten: other step back.]*
                I shield thee securely, in bliss for to be,
                And name thee as Lucifer, bearer of light.

GABRIEL: All bliss is here dwelling about us:
                The while we are stable in thought

of a group of strangers, they are going to give an initial version of their role. It is likely that some of the actors will think other people in the room will be making some sort of rough and ready judgement on their performance. The director must be very sensitive to the stress that some (not all) actors will experience – especially for a young actor in a room with a well-known, experienced actor for the first time. The director must announce to the whole room exactly what it is they are hearing; that this is a first attempt at the whole play, with the actors taking chances, having worked on the play by themselves. The result will almost certainly have some rough edges and wrong decisions, but that is the reason why rehearsals are necessary; this is only the first step on the journey.

THE TIMETABLE FOR THE FIRST MORNING

The tried and tested formula for the first day is something like this.

10.00am

Full company call, plus other individuals (as described above), for coffee and general meet-and-greet. The director will be busy moving round the whole room making sure everyone is introduced to everyone else, exuding goodwill and confidence. S/he will also make sure that people who need to work closely together on something are introduced to each other. This could be among the actors, but as they will have so much time together, at this point the director will be making sure a particular actor meets the person who will be helping with a quick costume change. Or another actor might meet the set builder who can assure the actor that the set will be safe to climb up. Use this time to

OPPOSITE: Page of director's script with notes – shows director's notes on where lighting, slide and sound cues will probably be, plus odd jotting about the scene. BART FIUT

sort out practical worries, which are not to do with the text or character development.

10.30am

The director introduces the production. Everyone sits around a big table or on chairs in a circle, and the director welcomes everyone and introduces everyone. There is a common practice nowadays of people introducing themselves round the table, but I think the director can do himself a good turn by introducing everyone and mentioning their job. In the case of actors, the director should name their role and mention something about them. For example, 'John Mitchell who is playing Horatio, and we are lucky to get him because he has only just finished filming in Indonesia'. In the case of other people, saying a word about when and how the actors will meet with them would be useful. So, for example, 'This is Jean Harvey, fight director, who directed the fights for *Trafford Tanzi* in the West End and who will start with the Act Five fight tomorrow afternoon'; 'This is Paul from marketing who will want to talk to all the acting company at lunchtime about some publicity shots'.

After the introductions of the personnel involved in the production, the director will give an introductory talk about the play. This talk should include reasons for doing the play: 'I was interested in reviving this play because it seems very right for the times we are living in now. People are scared of the future and families are arguing with each other, so a play about civil war will resonate with the audience.' Or it could be as simple as, 'This is a very funny play with great characters and a small cast, which fits in perfectly with what the company needs to do at this time of year. It is very lucky that we are able to get Pauline in between her TV commitments, and we know already that it is doing well with advance sales.'

The director should then continue to outline the general approach, for example: 'I've chosen to set our production of *Julius Caesar* in contemporary times and the location could be Britain, but the place isn't the central thing about the play. The all-female casting is, of course, quite radical.' This talk is very important for everyone to understand the context of the details of the project. Leave a few moments for questions, but don't get drawn into details that will be sorted out in rehearsals. It is more important at this stage to answer questions from those people who are *not* in the cast, because it is very likely the director, whose priority will be in the rehearsal room, won't see some people concerned with the production again, for some time. The director should mention any special technical aspects of the show, for example: 'We will almost certainly be using strobe lighting and pyrotechnics in the production' or 'There will be a number of quick costume changes and wardrobe will come into rehearsals early next week'. The director should specify when and how people other than the actors can come into rehearsals. What is not acceptable are interruptions whenever anybody thinks of something. It is a good suggestion to say, 'I will always take a coffee break at about 11.00 and finish for lunch at 1.00. So catch me or the actors at those times. If you want to sit in on rehearsals you can [or cannot], but not until the second week' or something along those lines.

11.00am

Introduction by the designer. The designer should present the model of the set and the costume drawings. With some productions this might take only a short while because the action is set in one place and the costumes are all contemporary. With other productions it might be very involved, with multiple sets and many costume changes. The designer will talk about the ideas that underpin the design of the production, set and costume, as well as practical details: 'This costume is heavy and will be hot, so there will be a duplicate to change into at the interval'. It is often helpful to show illustrations from other sources that

have influenced the design, and if there is room for developments during rehearsal, say how much it might be possible to extend the design being presented. So, 'I wanted to get a feel of the sixties, so you'll notice little references to Andy Warhol in the costume design'. All the details from the director and the creative team are important for the actors to absorb, and equally importantly for marketing and the team making the costumes. In all this the director should act as the chairperson, asking questions and getting the best value out of the meeting for everyone's benefit. By the end of these two presentations, the room should have a strong background to the production and individuals will have had questions answered about their part in the production.

If necessary, the lighting designer, composer and fight director can also say a few words. It is important not to make the whole morning seem like a lecture, however.

11.30am

Start the read through – a vital time for the production. You want to get it off to a good start. You want everyone to feel they're involved in something good. There is a tendency for actors to cover the difficulty of the first read through by reading slowly, or quietly, or very casually. This doesn't help the play get off to a good start, so the director might employ some scheme to avoid this. It could be as simple as asking the actors to give it their best shot and read with energy and vitality. One tactic very commonly used is to allocate the actors any part to read, *except* the one they will be playing. This way no-one can judge an individual, the company get a good idea of the action of the play and later that day the actors, out of the spotlight, can read it again with their actual parts.

On the other hand, there can be something very exciting and inspiring about a good first read through, with the cast generating a real impression of what the final production will be like. If this model is followed, it is a good idea to tell the actors that you would like a spirited, energetic reading and not a neutral, restrained *sotto voce* reading.

The director should delegate a stage manager or someone with a small part to read out the stage directions, so that people in the room without a script can follow the action. In reading the play at home, actors frequently do not pay attention to the stage directions, so it is helpful for them too.

The interval in the play (assuming there is one) is the time to have a short break. The aim should be to have coffee, etc., ready. A stage manager should be able to prepare things for the break. It is a good idea to keep this break as short as possible, while allowing time for everyone to pick up a drink and take a comfort break. It is advantageous to keep going and not let the atmosphere of the world of the play get dissipated. With the break over, the director should move on to the second part of the play.

When the reading is over, the director should congratulate the actors, give them a warm seal of approval, thank everyone for their attendance, get the stage manager to remind everyone what they are doing next and take a lunch break. The optimum achievement is a good feeling all round, an understanding of the project and a sense of excitement shared by everyone in the room. On one side, and casually, the director needs to discreetly cheer up anyone who feels they didn't show their best side.

1.30pm

Lunch break. The director has the choice of staying with the actors or dealing with any issues thrown up by the read through. The latter is probably more likely because the read through often brings into focus questions that the team, who have already started on their work, have been thinking about. For example, the stage manager might say, 'I hadn't sensed in reading it at home just how quickly the actor has to get round to other side of the stage. This might be a problem on tour. We'll look out for

that.' The designer is very likely to want to check on set/props and costume issues, while the director should check that no one outside the actors has had any unforeseen surprises arising from the read through. Remember that the director will be busy in rehearsals from now on and there may not be a better time to have a quiet word with other departments. This is especially true if, as is often the case, the rehearsals are happening outside the theatre building, and if the wardrobe and set building are similarly dispersed. Take advantage of being able to get people to talk to each other. The director will very often have to act as the master of ceremonies to bring people together.

2.30pm

First rehearsal. From now on there are several different decisions the director might take. The following is an outline of the main options. With experience, every director will put together their own mixture of techniques and timetables for the rehearsal period.

There is a particular major doctrinal difference between directors. Some directors will want to get on with staging the play, giving it some shape, organizing the entrances and exits, getting a rough idea of the physical and emotional 'geography' of it, before going on to explore the text in detail, as the rehearsals progress.

Other directors will want to explore the text before the actors stand up and move. They will want to read through the play more than once, so that the cast have a very clear idea of the text. This is an approach derived from Stanislavski's system. They might then want to spend time 'actioning' the text (this is explained in Chapter 5).

Another approach is to start with improvisations based around the situations in the play. Rather than requiring the actors to make sense of the details of the text straight away, the idea is to map out both the main plot lines and relationships, and the emotional range of the play and characters.

CONVENTIONAL/ACTIONING/ UNDER-READING OR WHAT?

The most conventional route, adopted by directors like Richard Eyre, John Dove and Harry Burton, is to start straight away 'putting the play on its feet'. This means starting at the beginning of the play and putting into practice the broad ideas the director has thought about in preparation for the rehearsals. This involves the now-often-rejected notion of 'blocking'. This is working out the actors' entrances and exits, and the rough moves s/he might make in the action of the scene. In practice this is far less rigid than its detractors claim. The argument is that it restricts the actors' imagination because it is too early in the process for the actor to be able to say with certainty how the character would behave. While this is certainly an argument, it is often the case that, even after days of improvisations and explorations, the logic of the set or the action still demands certain staging requirements. In addition, it is only an interim decision and can be changed in a moment if it proves impractical. Having worked through the play, getting to know the rough shape of it, the idea will be to start again at the beginning and to constantly revisit every scene and build up layer after layer of detail, while analysing the text in greater and greater detail. Many actors enjoy the reassurance of a rough shape from the off. One of the questions that can amuse is an actor stepping onto the stage and asking the director, 'Am I here?' meaning, 'Is this the right place for me to come on from?'.

THE FIRST AFTERNOON – WORKING WITH THE CAST

An Outline Strategy

Here is a rough timetable for the conventional approach to rehearsals.

The director is now with the cast only and it is worth giving a clear explanation of how s/he is going to work during the rehearsal period. S/he might say something like: 'My approach will be to clarify the storyline this afternoon and, from to-morrow, simply work through the scenes in order. The first time through will be quite fast and simple. When we get through it, which I expect to do for the first time by Friday, we will go back to the start and devote more time to each scene so that we can work in close detail.' The first afternoon might be spent in reading the play again, together with a more detailed analysis from the director. It is not a good idea to spend a lot of time delivering academic speeches about the play, or about the writer, or about the social and political circumstances that influenced the writer. It is important – vital – to give the actors a clear background to the play; but actors are people who 'do'. Some will have an academic interest but, in general, actors are very practical. They want to know the general backdrop to the play. They will want to know what bits of research are necessary for them to create their character more accurately; they will want to know what is necessary to give a better performance. Many directors come from a university background, but the rehearsal room is a practical place where acting and directorial questions are asked and answered, rather than open-ended academic questions. It is not an Oxbridge tutorial. It needs very careful balancing to judge how much researched information is helpful. As a rule of thumb, it is probably true to say that most directors talk too much. This might be because:

- Like the actors, they are nervous at the outset.
- They have made a lot of decisions already, and the success of the whole enterprise is on their shoulders, and talking is a defence/delaying mechanism.
- They have done their research and want to hand on all the stuff they have found interesting.

There will be different approaches, depending on the category of the play. A new play or a little known classic will require the actors to 'discover' the play. A well-known play or one that has recently been successful will need less 'discovery'. However, even with well-known titles, such as *The Importance of Being Earnest* or *Twelfth Night*, the director should not assume that the whole cast are familiar with the details of the story. As theatre is the business of storytelling, it is a good idea for everyone concerned to know the story, and know it well!

One thing to understand is that for a director and many actors there is a two-way pull at the beginning. Both want to invent strategies to put off the moment of getting up and getting started, but at the same time both are keen to get started. Like going for a swim in the sea early in the year, take a deep breath and plunge in.

Actually Getting Started

One way of getting started is to do an 'up on your feet' run through, having done the read through in the morning. The actors take their own role and go through the whole play with speed and non-stop. The stage manager should call out who is coming on at the start of each scene. This should be light and frivolous with frequent exclamations by the actors of things like, 'Who am I saying this to?' and 'Of course, you're my sister!', as they start to discover the play. This can be a quick way of making the story clear to the cast, or at least some parts of the story clear to some people, and anything not fully understood can be the subject of further explanation. This is a good way of keeping everyone together on the first day, when there can be a sudden lost feeling in some cast members if they are not rehearsing in the afternoon of day one.

A Well-Earned Drink

Assume the first afternoon rehearsal will last until 5.00 or 5.30pm. On the first day, the director should have achieved introductions, a read through and a run through or second reading or blocking of the first few scenes. Next, you need to work out the following day's rehearsal with the deputy stage manager (DSM). Using the useful chart prepared before rehearsals started, it will be straightforward to make a rehearsal call, which the DSM will communicate to the cast – usually by texting and by posting a hard copy on the rehearsal room notice board or door, wherever the actors have been told to look.

The rehearsal call should contain the time when each section is to be rehearsed, the people involved in that section, any other simultaneous activity, such as a wardrobe call, music call, breaks in rehearsal and the end time. Conventionally the actors are referred to as 'Mr' and 'Ms'. Some people find this anachronistic but tradition, and indeed superstition, is strong in the theatre.

With the next day settled, the director can take the whole cast out for a drink. The director should pay for it personally. A bit of personal generosity can help set the tone for the rehearsals. Don't be the last to leave and, in the euphoria of having had a successful first day, don't make promises to the cast that can't be kept. The most frequent areas where a director might be tempted to fall in with an actor's requests are in promising that certain props or costume will be available in rehearsal. If they are central to the actor's performance, then the director will do everything to make it possible for the actor to rehearse with them; but sometimes there are delays, and the director should not risk losing the trust of the actors because of circumstances outside his/her control. Actors are naturally nervous about the production and their role in it, so keep seeing it from their perspective. The more you can create a feeling of security, the better. Small things count for a lot in the tunnel-vision world of the rehearsal room.

There needs to be a reliable source of boiling water, milk and sugar, tea and coffee. The stage manager should make it clear what system is being used for refreshments. Is the management going to provide tea, coffee and biscuits or are the actors going to put money into a kitty? This might sound very petty, but it is the cause of so much resentment that it pays to sort it out at the beginning.

DIAGONAL THEATRE COMPANY

THE COMEDY OF ERRORS WILLIAM SHAKESPEARE

REHEARSAL CALL FOR WEDNESDAY 22 NOVEMBER

10.00	FULL COMPANY WARM UP
	MR. BARROW TO WARDROBE FOR COSTUME FITTING
10.30	**ACT 5 SCENE 1**
	FULL COMPANY INCLUDING MR. BARROW
11.30	BREAK
11.45	**ACT 1 SCENE 1**
	MS. DUCKWORTH (Duke)
	MR. COKER (Egeon)
	MR. ROGERS (Goaler)
12.30	**ACT 1 SCENE 2**
	MS. MITCHELL (Adriana)
	MS. BEDFORD (Luciana)
	MS. Rowe (Dromio of Ephesus)
1.15	LUNCH BREAK
2.15	**ACT 2 SCENE 1**
	MR. WILKINSON (Antipholus of Syracuse)
	MS. GREEVES (Dromio of Syracuse)
	MS. MITCHELL (Adriana)
	MS. BEDFORD (Luciana)
	MR. Rowe (Dromio of Ephesus)
	MR. COKER TO WARDROBE FOR COSTUME FITTING
3.30	BREAK
3.45	FULL COMPANY TO WATCH MARX BROTHERS FILM
5.30	REHEARSAL ENDS

REMINDER: Full Company off the book by Monday 27 November

Thank you.

David Jackson
Stage Manager

Rehearsal call sheet. A typical rehearsal call sheet indicates rehearsals and other activities, such as costume fittings.
BART FIUT

A Quick Chat with the Designer

It is usually the case that the first day brings into clear focus a number of things, which either hadn't been thought of or which were deliberately left until the actors had started. It is, therefore, essential to liaise with (at minimum) the designer, production manager and stage manager at the end of the day. Here you will discuss things like what to do about the scene where, in the action of the play, some actors eat a meal on stage, but one of the actors has revealed an allergy problem. Having seen the actors together, maybe the idea of one actor lifting up another one seems unrealistic, so what will happen instead? The director must be flexible and practical; willing to change things, but understanding at what point the production will be compromised.

THE SECOND DAY AND THE REST OF WEEK ONE

The most straightforward way to proceed on the second day is to start at the beginning of the play, if the first afternoon was a second read through or a run through. The director should have worked out the staging for the obvious events in the play; this includes entrances and exits. The logic of the entrances and exits is going to be more specific in a play with an interior setting (a Chekhov or Ayckbourn play) than in a more poetic or abstract play. The director will have decided on the layout of the 'off-stage' world. The actors also need to know where the furniture, if used, will be positioned. It is important to have substitute tables and chairs in what are likely to be the best positions, because the actors need to imaginatively make the room their own. The first time working through the play will iron out the basic logistics and will have answered some questions about the characters' behaviour. The speed at which the director takes the cast through the play will vary with the type of play. A contemporary play, many of which are short, might take two days. A classical play, like a Shakespeare, will easily take twice as long. If actors get anxious that they are not getting the chance to discuss difficult passages, ambiguous relationships, subtext and so on, they must be reassured that the opportunities for close analysis will come when everyone has had a chance to understand, in general terms, what they have to do.

One of the trickiest things to grasp is how much time to allocate for each scene or section. The first time though, in week one, you can probably make a reasonable guess, depending on the number of pages and the complexity in terms of number of actors in the scene. Look carefully at what happens on day two and judge from that how long the next day's section will take. Be aware that some actors might feel they are being rushed through, but most will like getting an overview. The director needs to keep an eye out for the actor who looks worried and needs reassurance.

THE SECOND WEEK

Assuming the rest of week one is spent making a broad brushstroke journey through the play, the next stage, in the second week, will be to go from the start again. The director will schedule much more time on each scene or section for vital discussion of the details of the scene. It is a good idea to tell the actors that they need to be off the book (i.e. lines to be learnt) after this second look at the scenes. During this second rehearsal, the director can discuss what the characters have been doing prior to their entrance; what they want to achieve in a particular scene; what are their biggest obstacles to obtaining their goals; and how the character sets out to achieve their goal – the basic series of questions of the Stanislavski system. However, the director must be very aware that the rehearsal is not an acting class. In a rehearsal with experienced actors, the director will assume that the actors have already made decisions about their character and they are quite likely not to want to discuss it much. However, if an actor is offering something that is *against* the text, then the director is duty bound to discuss what the thought process has been to reach that conclusion.

Only experience can teach the director how much discussion is valuable and when it is time to draw the conversation to a close. One guiding principle is that doing is almost always more instructive than talking. The director or one of the actors suggests a new way of doing the scene. Someone says something like, 'Maybe character X comes on suspecting that her husband is already fancying my character?'; the director's job is to put this idea into practice. 'It will mean the other characters will have to react differently. Think how you will react.' And so they try it out and incorporate anything and everything that makes the story clearer.

In the end every director will evolve their own approach to rehearsing, balancing theory with practical experience. Whatever methods are employed, it is important the director keeps the rehearsal process positive with a sense of moving forward with new discoveries or consolidation day by day.

7
LATER REHEARSALS

DEALING WITH THE CAST

Rule number one for the director is not to have favourites in the cast. While it is accepted that leading actors, or more well-known actors or senior actors, will get more attention in rehearsal than the newly graduated actor taking a small role, the job of the director is to make everyone feel they are noticed and that their contribution is important. The director needs to be even-handed with every member of the cast.

Take a Break

There can sometimes be a kind of obsessive quality about rehearsals, where the actors and the director feel it is better to keep on going under any circumstances. It is as if everyone believes that the sheer number of hours will make a good production. It is true that long hours and hard, consistent work are needed to rehearse a show successfully. However, it is counter-productive to rehearse *ad nauseam* with no clear objective in mind. Equity, the actors' union, has successfully campaigned to fix regular breaks and negotiated working hours for rehearsals and for performances. These should be adhered to, even in circumstances where the actors are not working to an Equity contract. The director will be in a much stronger position to ask actors for a favour (if it were needed) if s/he has worked to the regulated hours. It is part of the basic qualities of good directing – gain and keep the trust of the actors.

It is also important to be able to rehearse both seriously and with a light touch. No one likes a director who constantly behaves as if the play is the most serious thing in the world, but on the other hand, constant flippancy will undermine the rehearsals. It is a fact that the mood and behaviour of the director will set the mood of the rehearsal; so it is no help if the director brings in all the cares of their private life or a bad mood generated by something outside the boundaries of the rehearsal. The director is quite within his/her rights to expect the same from the members of the cast. If an actor or stage manager is bringing their own depression into the room, then the director must address it. Rehearsal time is always precious and there is no time to be wasted while everyone gets caught up in one person's misery. Obviously the case is very different if an actor has just heard bad news; but simple moodiness is not allowable.

Getting off the Book

One of the most frequent problems with actors is getting the lines learnt. Having the script in hand can be a reassuring defence mechanism. Cancelling the rehearsal is an acute solution. More usually, peer pressure from other people in the scene is enough to get a recalcitrant actor back on track. At other times the stage manager can be used to pass on a message that the director has in the past refused to re-employ actors who failed to learn their lines on time.

The *Deloitte Ignite Festival* at the Royal Opera House had 'Forests' as a theme. A walk-through installation of old opera costumes with animal heads was created by Jane Janey Design. JANE JANEY DESIGN

NON-AVAILABILITY

Another frequent difficulty that arises in rehearsal is non-availability. This happens most frequently in opera, but it is often the case, in any rehearsal, that an actor will want time off to audition or to fulfil an engagement that – it is claimed – predated the current engagement. Strictly speaking the agent should have declared any prior engagements before the contract was signed. It is a good idea when offering the part to ask the agent if there are any NAs (non-availabilities). However, auditions often come at short notice. If the director agrees too readily, then there is a chance it will be the excuse for other cast members to ask for time off. The director should tell the actor that it is not convenient to allow time off during the day (unless of course it is easy to accommodate) and can a time when the actor is not rehearsing be found. In the end the director is likely to let the actor go, but it is worth making the point that the actor is contracted to the current management and it is only goodwill that is letting the actor go.

Sensitive Scenes

Despite wanting to appear in front of strangers as someone not themselves, actors are often very nervous about looking foolish. This often revolves round a costume that the actor does not feel comfortable in, or in doing something potentially embarrassing on stage, like taking off some article of clothing or doing a scene with sexual content. The director's response must be full of sympathy. If it is just a matter of an actor taking off a shirt and he is anxious about having a fat stomach on view, a bit of gentle cajoling often works. A decision might have to be taken on how important the potentially embarrassing moment is to the action of the piece. The likely audience is also a consideration if it is a question of strong language or nudity. The style of the production will also be a consideration – a stylised idiom is generally easier to change than pure naturalism. The director should have anticipated the hazard and be ready with alternatives or good reasons to persevere.

A scene with sensitive content would be a perfect opportunity for an improvised game. Four chairs are arranged like a car and the situation is that three people are driving along and pick up a hitchhiker. The hitchhiker has some particular quirk and the idea is that this is slowly revealed and is at first resisted but gradually 'caught', in turn, by the other people in the car. So, for example, the director can instruct the first hitchhiker to be a person who can't stop using the word 'cigar', and replaces place names or people's names with 'cigar'. At first the passenger next to him in the back seat corrects him but gradually gets infected, and then on to the front-seat people. Another might only talk on words that begin with the letter B. The next hitchhiker can be a woman who is obsessively worried about if she locked the house door. The next hitchhiker can be someone who is always trying to take their shirt off.

The problem of embarrassment most often comes up in serious plays, not in a comedy or farce. If a serious scene requires the actor to appear nude or semi-nude, then the director must have explained that at the audition stage. The actor is, therefore, well aware that it is a requirement of the role. When the rehearsal of that scene is scheduled, the director must ask the actor how s/he would like to proceed. Would the actor like the rehearsal room to be closed to everyone except other characters in the scene and the director? Would the actor prefer to have only the characters who speak in the scene? Is it OK if the stage manager is there? The director can assure the actor that the window blinds will be pulled down, or whatever is necessary to make the room private. Whatever the circumstances, the director must understand that this can be a testing moment and utmost discretion is needed around this issue. It is usually much more embarrassing in rehearsal than in performance, where the lighting and the set and the conviction of the character make it, counter-intuitively, a more private thing.

Taking the Tough Decisions

Occasionally actors disagree on issues in the play and its interpretation, or on issues outside the play. It is one of the less pleasurable things a director has to deal with. An actor might complain that another actor has been drinking before going on stage. The director must not immediately make assumptions but, if complaints are found to be true, the director must intervene for the sake of the other actors and the production. In serious cases it might involve the union; in extreme cases it might involve dismissal. If an actor's behaviour is dangerous towards other actors, it might mean instant dismissal or at least suspension. In less serious cases it might just need a stern word from the director. But whatever the degree of seriousness, the director must not avoid dealing with an antagonistic situation.

ACTIONING AND OTHER APPROACHES

For some directors the conventional approach outlined above fails to give the actors sufficient insight into the text and can lead to subtleties of the subtext being overlooked. In response, a different approach has evolved. Instead of plunging straight in and working the text and the staging simultaneously, this method starts the rehearsals with a detailed analysis of the text; then, fanning out from that, the subtext, the character motives and the other broadly based Stanislavski system of ideas. In particular, a technique called *actioning* has become very widely used in this country.

Actioning is marking the text with a transitive verb for each line, so that every line is defined with a transitive verb. The idea is that the actor builds up a list of active verbs that describe what the character is thinking line by line, so that every line can be illuminated by precise knowledge of what the character wants to achieve. Each actor can then be precise about what his or her character is doing to the other character or characters in the scene. The result is that every line has a purpose

---

ACTIONING

Jim: Why are you doing this exam?
Challenges
Sue: I'll get a pay increase if I pass.
Enlightens
Anyway you'll benefit too.
Soothes
Jim: Are you still being underpaid?
Interrogates
Sue: I'm at the top of my grade.
Corrects

---

and the text is vitalized. Marina Calderone produced a book of transitive verbs, *Actions – The Actors' Thesaurus*. Here is an example:

Each character has an objective (something that they want for themselves) and the actions are the means by which they try to achieve this. The action must always be to affect someone else, not oneself. That is why they are transitive – they transform the behaviour of the other person.

Benefits

The overwhelming advantage of this method is that by the end of it, each actor has in his/her script a line-by-line, or at least sentence-by-sentence, analytical guide to everything their character says. This should enable the actor to unambiguously give purpose and direction to their lines, and with that a sharply defined portrayal of their character. The process is hard because working out what verb is appropriate for every line is not easy. However, the end result is that, with knowledge of the intention of every line, the performance is very active, truthful and compelling. It is an antidote to generalized, vague and un-thought-out acting, which can come from making easy assumptions about the text. The director is able, in conference with the actors, to more easily orchestrate the performances.

Actioning can give a strict focus on the other actor(s) in the scene, as well as forcing the actors to be precise in the choices they make in performance. It can expand the range of acting options by making the actor think carefully about possible choices that could be contained in the line.

The next step after actioning the text is to investigate the appropriate activities that will support the action described in the transitive verb. So, for example, the transitive verb that best suits the line from *Julius Caesar*:

Friends, Romans, countrymen. Lend me your ears!

could be 'I implore' you or 'I beg' you. In this case, a simple gesture might be appropriate, or the use of a prop or a pause. This is a simple and obvious example, but it illustrates the point that physical action stems from psychological impulse. There is not going to be a gesture for every line but at least there has to be consideration of the possible activity. The link to Stanislavski is that he wrote about the link between emotional and psychological experiences and precise, physical actions.

Drawbacks

The problem with this approach is that, in the first place, every actor has to be sure that they know what a transitive verb is. Having learnt about verbs, the process of going through a whole play line by line and agreeing what the best and most appropriate transitive verb might be is very long, and can be tedious. It can be quite quick with a modern play, but with a classical play it is very time-hungry. Literally weeks of the rehearsal period can be spent sitting at the table discussing and deciding on the actioning. Of course the actors develop a comprehensive knowledge of the play through this method, but it can worry some actors that they are not progressing with building the performance in the conventional way. The profession is divided on this approach. Many directors – Marina Calderone, David Thacker and Adrian Noble – are keen on this analytical approach, and it has certainly produced very many memorable and dazzling productions. If a director decides to adopt this method, they must be very sure how to implement it. Some actors will find it uncomfortable, and will need the reassurance that the director is confident and knows exactly what they are doing.

Detractors of this method say it can produce rather cerebral performances; if the reaction and response to a line from another actor is predetermined, it can inhibit a truthful response. If the response is pre-planned, the actor perhaps does not pay attention to the other actor. A play text is already selective and the individual actor's response to his or her fellow actors is a way of giving the text vitality.

There is plenty of opportunity to learn about this approach. Look up the informative *Workpack*, contained in the Out of Joint company's website, in the first instance, to see how he describes it in detail.

UNDER-READING AND ITS VARIANTS

It is interesting that those who have used a particular method of rehearsing usually loudly applaud it. The director Glen Walford, who has a very distinguished record as both a freelance and an artistic director of theatre companies, has evolved a very interesting approach to rehearsing. The actors do not have copies of the play, at least not in rehearsal, but she feeds the actors the lines and they repeat them as they hear them. Actors who work with her have praised the liberating effect in rehearsal of not having to struggle with the lines first, which puts on hold exploration of the physical aspects of the character or scene. Without a book in hand, the actor is free to move and explore and, of course, to listen carefully to the other actor's lines, which with book in hand often becomes of secondary importance.

This method has been, perhaps, more formalized through Tessa Schneidemann, and from her through Brian Astbury. This method is called under-reading. Again, the actors are freed from holding a copy of the play; instead each actor has a shadow actor, or reader, who feeds the actor the lines in small instalments. Freed from conventional book reading, the actor can explore all other elements of the scene. Difficulties that immediately suggest themselves – how does the actor hear their own lines when the other actors are being fed their lines at the same time? How can it be anything but staccato if the actor is waiting for the lines to be served up in seven-word chunks? In practice, the evidence is that these problems simply do not arise. In fact our hearing is selective in everyday life, so the actor can distinguish the lines intended for him/her. A variation is to record the lines, although this might not adapt to the varying speed of delivery as the rehearsal progresses. Phelim MacDermott and others have used this method successfully, and a set of basic rules has been evolved and listed by Astbury in his book *Trusting the Actor*.

IMPROVISATION

A long-established and familiar method is to devise scenarios for improvisation. This useful method can clarify the intentions of the actors in a scene, and they can return with more confidence to the actual text, having explored the emotional content of a parallel scene using their own language. Again, it is a way of freeing the actor from the limitations that are sometimes perceived by concentrating solely on the printed word. Improvisation can also make the relationships between characters more clearly defined. Improvisations often work well in rehearsing a classical play where actors have to overcome the unfamiliarity of the text, and then bring out, truthfully, the emotional content of the scene. The actors can use their own words, becoming more certain of the emotional direction of a scene. Very often in an improvised scene the language and the situations can become exaggerated, which is useful for defining the limits of the scene. With a classical play or a complex modern play it can be very useful to set up improvisations that simply make the plot clear to everyone. It is fun to ask different groups to take a section of the play and present it in different styles – melodrama, comedy, musical.

Improvisation in its many forms is well documented, but it is worth making the point that for it to work effectively as an aid to understanding a play and the characters, the director needs to set it up with clearly defined objectives. There needs to be a discussion afterwards, so everyone involved can understand the positive outcomes. There is always a temptation to make improvised scenes either highly emotional or comic. Actors and director must understand that the aim of the improvisation is to clarify the scene, the action and relationships. It is not an entertainment in itself.

If the director is going to use improvisation in rehearsals – and it can be a very useful tool – then it is a good idea to run some at the start of rehearsals. By doing all the funny and comic stuff, it can be got out of the way. Also, do some serious improvisation. Allow some not to be great in terms of a story, but to illustrate a point. They don't *all* have to be perfect gems!

DAVID MAMET

In his book *True or False: Heresy and Common Sense for the Actor*, David Mamet challenges the whole notion of using Stanislavski's system for creating character and understanding a play. He challenges the generally accepted view that rehearsal is an investigation into emotion and relationships.

He emphasizes that the character is an actor, not an invented 'other being'. Mamet is definite in his view that all an actor needs to know are the lines and where to go on stage. He calls Stanislavski a dilettante theorist and denounces his method as nonsense. Actors, argues Mamet, should ditch books about the text. If you want to act, give up study and just go out and do it. He contends that actors only need to say the words as simply as possible, with as little interpretation and characterization as possible. While his views run counter to accepted practice, any director ought to read his provocative book and think about his approach.

SHAKESPEAREAN REHEARSAL PRACTICE

As already mentioned, at some time or another the director is going to direct a Shakespeare play. Some particular conditions apply to rehearsing a play in a semi-foreign language.

Shakespeare writes of 'the two hour traffic of the stage'. However, most productions today last three or more hours. Why is this? The speed of delivery today tends to be quite slow, the idea being that because the text is dense and unfamiliar it is better to give the audience a bit more time to understand it. The director must work to oppose this natural instinct, which most actors have learnt somewhere. For evidence of how quickly and easily an audience can understand Shakespearean blank verse, listen to the work of Northern Broadsides in full throat. Their quick-fire delivery binds the sentences and thoughts together in a way that is lost when the production aims to explain everything by careful, deliberate delivery. With Broadsides, because of the speed of delivery, the subject of the sentence is closer to the verb, for example, and the northern vowel sound often completes rhymes that are lost in received pronunciation (RP). Their production of *Richard III* was about two hours. The director should pick up the actors if they are leaving unnecessary pauses.

The key thing the director must work on in rehearsals of Shakespeare is making sure the actors speak in sentences. The speeches are laid out on the page following the blank verse, and the sense often carries on through several lines. If any actor is adopting the habit of stopping at the end of each line, regardless of the sense, it is often a good idea to set the cast the task of writing out some of their part as if it were prose – not blank verse. With the words arranged in a way that looks like a novel or a modern play, the actor frequently finds it easier to convey the sense. Another helpful trick is to get the cast to walk while speaking

---

How Different it Would Have Been at The Globe Theatre

It is interesting to remind ourselves how Shakespeare's plays were originally rehearsed.

- The writer produced the full script, which was assessed by The Master of the Rolls; any content regarded as scandalous or dangerous was censored.
- In the same way as an orchestral player today is given only his or her part to play in a concert, the actors were given their script, which was only their part. There was only the cue line as their prompt, to indicate where in the play the lines would be spoken.
- The level of concentration would have been very intense; almost everything we now think of as important in a rehearsal – truth of character and emotional values – would have been very difficult to achieve.
- The audience and performers today expect different qualities from those that the original audience would have appreciated. Shakespeare was famous in his own day but, we may assume, for the plots and language rather than as now, when it is the details of the production and character that are most commented on.

their lines and then make a turn whenever there is a change of thought. The actor should aim to find as many twists and turns in the speeches as possible.

The speaking of Shakespearean verse often becomes tedious and repetitive, with the actors taking too much notice of every piece of punctuation – misled by the arrangement of the blank verse on the page and pausing at the end of every line. The actor needs excellent breath control and variety of delivery. The director should remind the actor that it is important to identify the construction of the speech. Are there any examples of antithesis? Any alliteration? Is there a list, because in a list there is an opportunity for the actor to choose a most liked and a most disliked item on it? Look at the John Barton's master classes. As a matter of course, get the actors to speak the verse in an American accent (or Italian, or French, or Yorkshire or Scottish) – any accent will do. Get them to listen to the cadences they use in an exaggerated New York accent, and let it invigorate their old RP.

In a Shakespeare play, the director is very likely to encounter stage combat. The fight director must be given a lot of time and regularly scheduled rehearsals, so that the moves in the fight become completely automatic. The actors can act the narrative of the fight, but they must *never* be left to improvise the actual moves with weapons.

NOTES AND NOTE GIVING

The notes' session is a very important part of the rehearsal process. It is here that the director sits in front of the production as a member of the audience, while imagining the event from the writer's and actors' points of view simultaneously. Just as different members of an audience might voice a variety of reactions, so the director's notes can be far-ranging. Directors often think they must become great theatre gurus in the notes' session, but the key is to be practical. The director must try and hear the text as if for the first time.

NOTES - DRESS TUESDAY

1. noise in wings before start.   *(Self explanatory)*
2. LX 2 late. Go with sound.   *(put lighting cue 2 at same time as sound cue)*
3. JH - trousers!   *(something very wrong with costume. Too big)*
4. SQ 4 up.   *(sound cue 4 needs to be louder)*
5. All - stop fading at end of lines. Pick up cues! *(perhaps the most common faults)*
6. Sue - present the prop. Let us see the knife *(audience need to see clearly)*
7. P7. LB louder.   *(actor on page 7 speak up)*
8. Still too quiet!   *(same actor still too quiet)*
9. LX 8/9 slower. Wait for soldiers to exit *(two lighting cues to go slower and change cue point)*
10. AR 'elephant' n/a.   *(actor not audible on single word)*
11. Neil get to piano earlier. Be ready!!   *(actor probably worked this out for himself)*
12. Redo LX 20. Go darker. Bluer.   *(darker blue for lighting cue 20)*
13. NO! MR we changed your entrance to s/r *(slight annoyance creeping in, come on stage right)*
14. SM set beer crates more s/l *(stage management to put beer crates more stage left)*
15. Words of 'Tonight you are going to see' LEARN! *(annoyed, this has been rehearsed)*
16. Restage p. 24/25. Can't see MC   *(director's error, an actor not visible)*
17. Design finish paint beer wagon *(design team to be reminded to finish painting wagon)*
18. Production eta masking?   *(Production manager to sort out the masking)*
19. Props. Mask?   *(Props person where is the mask?)*
20. Slide 15 wrong.   *(Self explanatory)*

Page of director's notes. The director will write down a wide variety of comments, from the subtle to the mundane.
BART FIUT

WHAT AND WHY IS RP?

- Most plays are spoken in the voice or accent called received pronunciation (RP).
- Shakespeare, in particular, attracts the RP voice, although the plays were never originally spoken in that voice.
- RP is the self-confident voice of the Victorian British Empire. The development of the term RP coincides with the growth of the empire in the late eighteenth and nineteenth centuries.
- Shakespeare is spoken in RP because it became a fashionable idea that the socially elevated characters should speak with an upper-class voice.
- The hallmarks of RP are a literal stiff upper lip, an evenness of delivery (a minimum of up and downs in the speech) and a falling away at the end of the sentence.
- In many ways it is ill-suited to the delivery of heroic blank verse: it particularly adversely affects the end of sentences.
- The director must constantly watch out for actors failing to carry the energy to the end of the line.
- For comparison, get the actors to speak their lines in broad American accents.

Text

Are there individual words that are not clear? Are there sentences that require better articulation from the actor? Are they saying what is on the page? Are they committing the (almost inevitable) English actors' mistake of letting the words sink down vocally and emotionally at the end of the line?

Staging

Are the actors always in the best place on stage to deliver their lines? In the push for ultra-naturalism, directors have sometimes placed the actors in a traditional proscenium arch (sometimes called 'end on') staging with their backs to the audience, even when delivering important lines. The writer has written his lines to be heard and understood. The audience have paid to hear those lines. Don't let the production deny them this simple pleasure.

Plot

Essentially acting is about storytelling. The director is there to ensure the story is clear. When the director can more or less see what the finished article will look like, s/he must be sure the story is

clear. When we first meet characters, we must be clear of their relationship to each other. We must be clear about the location. The director should remind the actors to give great clarity to names of people and places the first time they are mentioned. 'What country, friend, is this?' 'This is *Illyria* lady.'

Pacing

Successful theatre is all about shrinking time. If the play lasts ninety minutes, but it feels as if it lasts for only half an hour, then it's a success. If it lasts for half an hour but it feels like ninety minutes, then it's not a success. One of the basic faults in many otherwise good productions is that the audience get to the end of the line before the actor has spoken the words. Given the context and the character, is often easy to predict what the character is going to say. The actor very often, out of negligence or good manners, or some other reason, hesitates before speaking their line. Witness what happens in real life by listening to the recording of a birthday or Christmas party. Even in a formal setting sitting around a table, the microphone picks up every conversation indiscriminately. The result is a series of overlapping conversations. The listener has got the idea of how a sentence will end and jumps in either over the speaker or bang on the end of the speaker. In a play there is – all too often – the minutest pause before the speaker replies. It can produce a very dull scene or exchange.

Overall, has the director got variety of pacing? Are the speedy parts of the story being told speedily? Are the meditative parts being given sufficient space to breathe? Often actors and directors respond to text in particular way because of some 'invisible tradition'; so, Chekhov is often approached in a slow-moving idiom. Some of the leading characters are idle, middle-aged, lost in an unsatisfactory marriage, full of yearning and melancholia: all of which can encourage a listless staging and delivery. It is as well to remember that people are often very busy and energetic when their lives are full of frustrations. They might be inwardly angry and resentful, rather than lethargic.

Is the play too long? Should it be edited down? Should it be played as one continuous piece for two hours or should there be an interval? As the rehearsals proceed, the director needs to be asking questions the audience might ask. It is useful to remember that no audience ever (or only extremely rarely) left the theatre complaining that the play was too short. Or too clear. Or too funny. Or too moving.

Character

Are the characters convincing? Are they balanced between each other? Is a more minor character dominating a scene by doing extraneous business? Do all the characters inhabit the same world? The stage is a metaphor, not a real place, but we, the audience, have to recognize enough about the consistency of that world to have a relationship with it. Do the characters belong together in that world? Are any of the characters too similar to each other? The director should create variety within speeches and between the characters.

Timing

In all drama, but especially in comedy, it is important to time with absolute precision the actors' responses, entrances, pauses, stage business and so on. Comedy is about sharpness – sharp entrances and exits. Not just the moment and speed an actor makes the entrance or exit, but also the way the set is constructed. The comedy actor needs a sharply defined doorway or a hard flat, not a loose-hanging drape (unless there is business about the drape). The sharp edge is a reminder of how comedy works to a large extent. Popping open a bottle or can needs to be precisely timed. It must not muddy or obscure important dialogue with noisy business or movement.

An actor must learn to hold for a reaction. Hold back on a character's reply: it can be funny when the actor says what the audience is anticipating. Sometimes it is better to come in *immediately* if the response is going to be a surprise. The director must at all times keep the action clear and clean.

Playing to Strengths

It is important that the actors are simultaneously challenged to do more, go further, act more bravely; but, at the same time, it is equally important that the actors also use the best gifts and abilities they have. Does the production allow the actor with the great voice to show it? Or the one who is athletic to demonstrate it? Of course it will depend on the nature of the play whether these things can be accommodated; but if they can, then let the audience's pleasure be enriched by them.

The play is approaching the final stages of rehearsal and special attention must now be paid to the transition from rehearsal room to the stage.

8

FINAL REHEARSALS AND OPENING NIGHT

If you have had three weeks to rehearse, you will have spent week one with the read through and briefly working through the whole play, and week two with a detailed rehearsal of the play, culminating with a run through (it might have been called a 'stagger through' to take the edge off the worry of the title 'run through'). If the director has applied the actioning technique, you will have spent longer sitting and studying the play, and the rehearsal period will necessarily have been longer. Similarly, if improvisation was a major part of the rehearsal, it would probably take a longer time. If you had four or five weeks, you will have been able to work through at a more leisurely pace, and have spent two or three weeks in looking at the play in detail.

However long the rehearsal process, it rarely seems long enough.

THE LAST FEW DAYS IN THE REHEARSAL ROOM

Assuming there was a run though at the end of the previous week, the priority for the start of the final week is to work through the notes the director made during that run. The play ought to be making sense. The individual performances should be clear. The story should be clear. What is most likely to need attention is the sense of forward momentum – the actors will still be feeling their way in some places. The director should not be afraid

of giving very simple notes on audibility and clarity of staging. In notes' sessions it is important not to blame the actors when it is not their fault. Rather than say to an actor, 'You're standing right in front of the person we most need to see at that moment' say 'I've carelessly placed you in the wrong place for that moment'. When something *is* their fault, don't be afraid to say so, but beware of embarrassing an actor in front of the rest of the cast. This is where a good sense of humour and a strong rapport built up during the rehearsals can really pay dividends. At this stage of the production you need to be able to efficiently and quickly make corrections and changes without upsetting anyone.

Monday and Tuesday of the Last Week

The director will want to work through the whole play again from the start, putting into action the notes from the previous Friday's run through. Some of the scenes will run straight through, but other scenes or parts of scenes will need more attention. The director will have worked out the schedule after the previous week's run, and Monday and Tuesday will be spent on this, the final work through.

Wednesday

On Wednesday the cast will be standing by for another complete run of the play. If the previous two days have gone well, this can take place in the morning, allowing some time in the afternoon for detailed notes. If a bit more time is needed for notes, then the run through will be on Wednesday afternoon. It is important to rehearse everything that is necessary before doing the next run. No actor will thank the director for doing a run with parts of scenes still in an unsatisfactory state, so make sure everything is fully covered before the next run.

Thursday

Again, the aim is to give notes and run the play for the third time. Before that, the director must give notes on the Wednesday run and attend to any bits that need special attention. The parts of the play that have gone well on both the previous week's run and on Wednesday can be left alone. In preparation for the Thursday, run any difficult and quick costume changes, rehearsed with who-ever is going to be helping with the changes. The inexperienced director needs to know that the first time set or costumes changes are attempted, they will take perhaps five times longer than when they have been streamlined, which happens by the team working out the most efficient order of doing things. The same is true of set changes for the first time in the technical rehearsal. In a production of mine, *The Plough and the Stars* (O'Casey), the first attempt at the set change was fifteen minutes for an in-view scene change! By opening night it was three minutes because of great organization.

Thursday afternoon will be the third run of the play, including the 'stagger through' the previous week. The set, costume, lighting and sound de-signers, and the production manager and stage management team, should come to watch it. The lighting and sound designers will have seen the model and spoken to the designer at the read-through day, and will have worked out the lighting and sound rig (the positions where the individual lights – often referred to as lanterns – and the speakers and mics, if used, will be hung or lo-cated). Now the lighting designer will check that he has everything in place to illuminate all necessary

---

SOME NOTES ON NOTES

- In all the notes' sessions, the director must be specific.
- The director must refer to particular, precise moments and lines, and be precise about what is necessary to happen at that point.
- A generalized note such as, 'Can you be more agitated?' is not as helpful as, 'The moment you see him entering, can you show your reaction by going through your pockets looking for the keys?'.

---

areas of the stage and to create the right moods, and in the same way the sound designer and the composer/musical director will want to check their areas of responsibility.

Everybody else connected to the show in a practical way should watch this run, with a sup-portive and generous attitude.

After the run, and before giving notes to the actors and stage management, the director will check with the lighting designer, fight director and costume supervisor if they have any questions or foresee any problems.

Friday

Work any bits that are still causing worry. Re-re-hearse costume changes and any other technical or musical moments. Depending on the schedule the company is working to, there will be a final run either on the Friday afternoon or the Saturday morning. Whenever the final run takes place, it is important that the cast leave with a positive re-sponse from the director.

PUTTING UP THE SET AND RIGGING LIGHTING AND SOUND

The timing of building the set and rigging the light-ing and sound equipment will depend on what else is happening in the performance space. The director will come into the space when the set is up and the rigging is complete to do the lighting and sound plotting; when that is completed, the cast will arrive and the technical rehearsal will start.

WALKING THE SET

Whatever the schedule, as soon as the set has been built the director should walk it to guess at any difficulties an actor might encounter. This might lead to minor alterations – a handrail being extended or an extra off-stage light in the wings. When the set is completed, then the sound and lighting plotting can be completed.

SOUND PLOTTING

The sound plotting is much quicker than the lighting plotting. In listening to the sound cues, the director needs to make a small allowance in volume for the difference when the audience are in the auditorium. Their bodies will absorb a small amount of the sound – say a maximum of 10 per cent. The sound plotting involves the director listening to each of the sound cues, and agreeing the volume level, duration and the direction of each of the sound cues. The director should give the DSM clear instructions on where in the action these cues will come and how they will finish. Will it be a fade out, an abrupt cut or a cross-fade into another cue?

PLOTTING THE LIGHTING

The lighting plotting is generally a much more complicated job; there are many more options. The director will work in harmony with the lighting designer to produce effective and atmospheric lighting for each scene and each special moment. The director and lighting designer must decide on the conventions they want to adopt. For example:

suppose a long scene is all set in the afternoon in a field, with a particularly dramatic moment halfway through it. Considering the scene naturalistically, there would be no change of light – it is a sunny day – but from a dramatic point of view, the emotional moment would be heightened if there were a lighting change. The decision has to be taken: should the lighting be entirely natural or will it follow the action of the play? Most directors would opt to follow the action of the play.

There was a fashion slavishly followed by The Royal Court Theatre in London to follow the convention of the Berliner Ensemble and light everything with even-intensity, open, white light, like a sports' event under floodlight. Today, directors like to use the full lighting resources.

With sound effects, music, lighting and video, there is a question of getting the right effect and not overburdening the play with too many technical devices. As a general rule it is better to have fewer than too many. A lot of unnecessary lighting cues can be very distracting, and the same applies to sound cues. The director should save up the undoubted high emotional punch that great sound or music connected with lighting can give the play: big moments are often undermined by too many fussy lighting cues.

Another aspect of lighting is the connection it has to the understanding of the text. It is always easier to understand what an actor is saying when his/her face is visible. There does not have to be a particularly bright light, but if the actor is in heavy shadow it is harder to focus on the character, and harder to understand or even hear them.

How Many Cues?

There is no set number of lighting cues. It will entirely depend on the kind of play in production, but it is probably best not to flood the play with overzealous lighting. As with other aspects of the show, it is artistically satisfying to have a sense of unity. The lighting designer will ask how quickly the lighting changes should take: three seconds is a

Melancholic scene from the opera *La Traviata*, recreated as part of Joanna MacGregor's *Deloitte Ignite Festival* at the Royal Opera House. This photograph shows the emotional impact lighting can achieve. TRICIA DE COURCY LING

good speed. Any faster and it becomes close to an instant change and slower starts to become a prolonged effect. The director at times will want faster and slower, but work outwards from a three-second fade.

If the action is returning to the same location and same situation as in a previous scene, the director can save time in plotting by restoring the existing lighting cue from the first time the action was in that place. The lighting plotting session

A FEW BASIC LIGHTING TERMS

- LX: shorthand for lighting; 'This is what LX 7 looks like'.
- State: the set-up of lighting for a scene or moment; 'This is the state for the duel scene'.
- Build: gradual increase of intensity of light but also refers to working on a state; 'Let's try building LX 5' meaning increase light; 'I am building LX 20' meaning I am working on creating LX 20.
- Cross-fade: the move from one state to the next – a time will be plotted for the cross-fade to take place; 'Cross-fade from LX 30 to 31 in five seconds'.
- Snap: instant change, usually for a black out.
- DBO: dead black out.
- Special: a single lantern for a particular moment.
- Birdies: little lights often used as footlights or fitted to the set.
- Restore: go back to previous lighting state.
- Cross-light: light coming from the sides.

Scene from the opera *The Saint of Bleeker Street*. A New York street in the early twentieth century. Another example of the mood effective lighting can produce. ARNIM FREISS

could last up to five or six hours or longer – so allow time. The DSM will note all the cue points in the prompt copy.

At the same time, the wardrobe will bring costumes to the dressing rooms and any costumes for quick changes into the wings, backstage areas or quick-change booth. The props manager will arrange the props table in the wings on either side of the stage or the most convenient places for props as the actors go onstage.

THE TECHNICAL REHEARSAL

The tech is one of the pinch points in the schedule, so it needs to be carefully considered. Wherever possible, time should be saved but not in a way that causes the actors to be anxious. Actors

worrying at this stage can be very time-consuming and morale-draining.

A word of warning. At the tech, and at the first dress rehearsal, it will seem as if the play the director has spent months planning, and weeks rehearsing, has been lost. The actors will be distracted by all sorts of new things. If everything has been properly planned and explained there should be no big surprises, but there will be very many details to absorb, such as timing entrances, paying attention to sound and lighting cues, working with the costumes or discovering the set is more difficult to manoeuvre around than it seemed in the rehearsal room, where there were no stairs, or levels or raked floors. Be assured that that the actors will get used to it all, but in the meantime a lot of the delicacy and subtlety that has been rehearsed may be lost for the time being.

THE TECH(NICAL) DAY

10.00am

Actors arrive and get into costume.

10.30am

The first thing the director has to do is to call the actors together in costume in the Green Room or in the auditorium, but not on the stage (too distracting to get full concentration), and explain the timetable for the day. The actors, however experienced, need to be reminded that having spent weeks in the rehearsal room, the set and the theatre will seem, for a short time, an unfamiliar, even a hostile place. Remind the cast that the feeling will pass and the new environment will feel like home in a few hours. Also remind the cast that the acoustic is going to be different and they will have to adjust their playing accordingly. It is useful to tell the actors not to assume that a scene when finished will not be run again for a scene change; so actors should always stay on stage until the tech has clearly moved on to the next scene. A huge amount of time is lost when actors leave the stage and go back to a dressing room or outside for a smoke. Finally, the director must remind the cast that tech is a difficult time for everyone; although they have been living the play for several weeks, this is the first time for the technical crew. The message to everyone is be patient and keep calm! The director must explain how s/he intends to run the tech.

RUNNING THE TECH – OPTIONS

There are really only two options for running the tech. First, the tech can be used to answer every single question and sort out exhaustively each problem. In this kind of tech, a quick costume change will be done as many times as is necessary to get it absolutely right. The director wants to be certain that it will run completely according to plan in the dress rehearsal; the same with the

lighting changes. The director wants to be certain that the lighting will happen precisely on cue. In this case, the tech will take several days, but at the end the director will have seen everything working precisely and accurately.

The other option, which perhaps only comes with experience, is to push on with the tech. Adopting this option, the director is implicitly thinking of moving efficiently through the tech, maybe with the very occasional thing not running to perfection, but well enough, in order to get to the first dress rehearsal, where in a non-stop situation the real problems, if any, can be identified. In the case of a quick costume change, for example, know it will speed up the more it is done. If the first time it is five seconds too long, talk to the actor and the quick-change helpers and ask if they think it will go five seconds faster next time. If the answer is yes, then move forward. The same with cueing. If the DSM is late with a cue, rather than stopping everything, wait a moment until the cued change is over and ask the DSM if it would be advisable to repeat the sequence to get that one cue in place. Very often the DSM will answer that it was late for a reason that can be easily fixed, and it will not happen again.

The director must let everyone know what preferences s/he has for running the tech and then go to the production desk, while the actors stand by. The production desk will be set up in the middle of the auditorium with spaces for the director, the designer, the lighting designer, sound designer and composer, if there is one. The lighting designer will be connected on cans (headphones) to the lighting board operator and the sound designer to the sound operator. The director should have cans so as to be able to hear when cues are given. This can save a lot of time because the director can tell if a cue is wrong, if it was the cue being late or the operator missing the cue, or anything else. If there is a simple explanation, then there will be no need to stop the tech. It is *imperative* that the director keeps as quiet on the cans as possible. Everyone else is dealing with a new production and the last thing they need is any reprimand or bad mouthing from

FIVE IMPORTANT REMINDERS ABOUT 'THE TECH'

- The cast of the play will often want the tech to be a sort of dress rehearsal.
- It is the first time the technical crew have had to work with their part of the show.
- The director must remind the actors that this is not their rehearsal.
- The director must remind the actors that it is possible either to view the tech as an exciting part of the process or to think of it as boring and exasperating. The expectation is that they will view it as the former.
- The expectation is that everyone will be patient and polite.

the director. The director's headphones are really for listening in and the occasional question. In the tension of the moment it is too easy for the director to get bad tempered, but this must be avoided or everyone will catch it, and progress will be badly compromised. The production manager will be onstage acting as liaison between the production desk in the auditorium and the stage – actors and crew.

Occasionally, the director will need to go on stage to listen to a problem from an actor or to see why a particular prop repeatedly causes difficulty.

The tech might start with a few moments for the actors to explore the set, although curious actors are likely to have sniffed around it already. Do not allow too much time for this exercise. Actors, being naturally anxious about the production, often start to invent difficulties with the set and with the costumes that do not, in fact, have any or much foundation. Of course the director must listen to actors, but needs to distinguish between real problems that will have to be solved before the technical rehearsal can start, and those imagined problems that will fade away as soon as the actors start to get used to their new surroundings.

11.00am

Very often, one of the trickiest parts of the tech is getting started. Some actor has a legitimate

reason for not being ready. The DSM does not get a clear response on headphones from the lighting, sound and stage crews, perhaps. But then everything is ready, and the first cues are called. The inexperienced director should not panic if the first sequences take time. Everyone is getting used to the new circumstances. Even old hands in that theatre are looking at a new set and a new production.

Once the tech is started, it will pick up speed as it progresses. What the director will want to achieve is knowledge that all the technical aspects of the show have been rehearsed. As outlined above, the more experienced director will perhaps not have seen everything run perfectly, but will have the instinct to know that it will be correct in the dress rehearsal. Mistakes or flaws are easily corrected by, for example, moving a cue or an actor getting round the back of the set a little bit quicker. Take a break at a sensible point, like the end of a scene, so that people coming back onstage after the break are not just coming back for a two-minute innings.

1.15pm

Break for lunch, with an extra fifteen minutes to get out of costume, and the same after the break to get back into costume. While the actors are unavailable for an hour and a half, the tech crew are free for half an hour after an hour lunch break to practise a set change; or the lighting designer can make alterations, now the actors are not on the set and a few adjustments need to be made. This is the moment a set of ladders or tallescope can be brought onstage for a spot of painting or lantern refocus.

2.45pm

Continue the tech. The old-fashioned calculation is that the tech should take three times longer than the play itself. The length of the tech will simply

A scene from Adrian Mitchell's play *Mind Your Head*. As the picture shows, the set was a double-decker London bus, with the front and back turned through 90 degrees. There was a rock band on the lower deck and the cast had to get used to the stairs to time their moves, and to play multiple parts with full costume changes. A very intricate tech. CAROL BAUGH

depend on the complexity of the production. In broad terms, the best approach is to keep it simple and save the technical magic for the big moments. As with the actors' performances, it is a question of variety and subtlety, alongside moments of extravagance and great passion. In the same way no-one wants actors shouting their way through a play, no-one wants over-played, attention-grabbing lighting, sound or musical effects.

Take breaks and work reasonable hours. This is not the moment to fatigue anyone – but the work must be completed. The priority is not to let a tech get out of control and jeopardize starting the first dress rehearsal on time.

Any physical aspects like dances, complex movement sequences and fights must be done *in full* during the tech. While a quick costume change or a lighting change can be left if it is within an ace of being correct, a dance or a fight or acrobatics must be thoroughly covered in the tech. Injuries from an unrehearsed movement sequence can end up with legal action!

The director, in making any decisions at the tech about repeating something, has to be thinking ahead to the first dress rehearsal. S/he should be thinking that if at the dress rehearsal something went wrong at this point, what would be the consequences? As said already, in the case of a slightly late lighting cue or a costume change taking a very few seconds longer, the consequences would be very slight; but in the case of a physical activity, the consequences could be very serious. Time will have been built into the tech schedule to allow for proper time on these activities. The tech for a musical will always be a lot longer than a straight play.

The director has an important job in keeping everybody calm. The actors and the director will feel strange, after weeks of close involvement, to be temporarily divorced. The designer, lighting designer and costume supervisor will feel anxious that their work is looking good and is what was intended; and the DSM has a lot to cope with, cueing everything and dealing with cue points that the director may well be changing because of the new circumstances of being onstage. In the middle of all these crosscurrents, the director must not add to their natural sense of worry by his or her behaviour. The director above all must exude a Zen-like calm that everything will be done as necessary and within the given timeframe. This is frequently difficult to do!

How to Ensure the Tech Runs Smoothly

- Good briefing – the lighting designer and sound designer should know what they are working towards.
- An efficient production manager and deputy stage manager – these two are the lynchpins of an efficient production week.
- Don't allow the tech to become an extra rehearsal for the actors – it is not their time. They must concentrate on their contribution to the technical aspects of the play, not the performance – yet.
- Work with the designer in the pre-production period on every aspect of the play, so there is no need for the designer to start thinking about redesigning at this impossibly late stage.
- The director should have had a photo or ground plans of the set all through the rehearsals, so there are no unpleasant discoveries just days before the opening.

10.00pm

The tech will take as long as it is scheduled to take. If it finishes early, then the stage crew have more time to tidy up their work. It seems there is always some bit of masking (hiding the off-stage areas with black drapes) or painting to finish. But it must be regarded as bad news if the tech over-runs. The rest of the run-up to the opening night will be seriously undermined. The tech will usually take until the latest time the cast can work to in the evening.

THE SECOND DAY

10.00am

If the tech is not completed on day one, then it ought to be finished by the mid-point of the second day. If it is completed, then everything can move forward by one rehearsal session. After the tech there will be things onstage that the production manager will need time to fix, so time must be given to the production manager to finish anything that needs attention; likewise, the lighting designer and the sound designer.

1.00pm

If the tech spilt into the morning, the production manager will still need time onstage to fix anything that went wrong at the tech. The wardrobe will have some alterations to attend to. This work will be done in the afternoon before the evening dress rehearsal. During that afternoon, the director can rehearse with the cast off-stage. The cast's experience, having spent a day and a half in costume and on the set, will inform this rehearsal, which might be about reminding the cast of the *details* of their performances, temporarily lost in the move to the stage. If there is a lot of modification to be done on stage, the director will take the actors to a rehearsal room to tidy up tricky moments.

6.25pm

The half-hour call for the dress rehearsal. Starting half an hour earlier than the normal show time allows a few minutes for urgent business before everyone goes home.

THE FIRST DRESS REHEARSAL

The director should remember that it is very likely that the first dress rehearsal will start with the actors being rather tentative. They have lost the security of the rehearsal room; they have lost the close physical contact between themselves and the director; and they are dealing with all the new aspects of the production – the set with doors and staircases perhaps, or the costumes, which may feel inhibiting, and the exact places they need to be in order to be lit effectively. It can feel quite lonely on the stage for an intermediate time as the actors acclimatize to the new environment. It is very often at this time that the beautiful, subtle moments, which the director cherished in the rehearsal room, get forgotten. If the technical aspects of the production are felt to be helping the production, then things will quickly fall into place. When the actor makes his/her second entrance, it should be with more confidence, with growing enthusiasm through the dress rehearsal. Things that are not helpful to the actor will become apparent. Furniture might need some rearrangement. The place that seemed right to house a prop turns out to cause small problems, so a stage manager might need to be on hand to help an actor quickly pick up a prop and so on.

At this point the director must hold on to everything that was good in the rehearsal room and not make wholesale concessions to the cast because (as they see it) some things are not feasible. The director should not say anything along the lines of, 'Let's see how it goes in the next dress rehearsal' because this is an invitation to the actor to demonstrate that whatever is the problem, it needs a radical solution. Rather, the director should be sympathetic and say something like: 'Yes, I see what's happening, but I think it's important, and it really adds to what you're doing if we can get it right. I'll put time aside to work on it.' If at subsequent attempts the problem does not get solved, then changes will have to be made; but it is the director's job to maintain everything that has been positively created in rehearsal.

THE THIRD DAY

10.00am

A lengthy notes' session with lots of detail from the director. The cast, DSM, production manager and lighting designer, movement director/choreographer and fight director should also attend the notes' session. The movement director and/or fight director can give their notes first, and then leave. The production manager is there on behalf of the technical team, and takes notes for them. It is useful to do all the verbal notes all the way through the play with the cast jotting down their personal notes. As the director goes through, s/he should write down the notes that need to be rehearsed in action, not just talking it through. The length of the notes' session should leave time to go back on stage and work through the bits that are causing concern. This should only be the specific moments and not spill over into a re-rehearsal of whole scenes.

The director will give full and detailed notes. These will include: all acting notes; audibility notes; staging and positioning notes; notes to do with getting in the right place to be lit properly; cueing notes – in fact, everything that is in the show. Although there may be long faces at a detailed and protracted notes' session, it is key that the director covers everything. There might only be one more dress rehearsal, so everyone must know what has gone wrong and how to fix it. There is an old superstition among actors that if someone praises something, it will not go that well again. It is good policy not to spend time on things that went correctly. Concentrate, in the time available,

on getting the mistakes ironed out. All the praise can come later. The director should tell the actors that the notes will pinpoint the things that went wrong; so, if something is not mentioned, the cast can assume it was right.

When jotting down notes, it is usually at speed because the director does not want to miss the action on stage. Notes are, therefore, very often difficult to read – and the cast do not want to wait while the director struggles to read his/her own writing. It is a very good idea to number the notes, then it will be easy to see where one note ends and the next starts. It is also heartening for everyone to see the number of notes reducing rehearsal after rehearsal, or vice versa!

It is a good idea to invent some sort of shorthand. It is not a good idea to use a Dictaphone or similar, because it will pick up every sound in the background and make the director's comments hard to hear. It is also more difficult to go back to a note. (The writer had a very embarrassing attempt to use a Dictaphone with terrible results!) It will also be difficult to find a dictated note if someone is missing from the session and it is necessary to repeat it.

PHOTOS

It is at this point that the marketing department will have arranged a photo call. The local, and sometimes the national, press will want to take production shots of the play. With a bit of good luck the photo will accompany the review. For this, the director needs to choose two or three strongly dramatic moments. If there is a locally popular actor or a nationally known actor in the cast, then the photos should include him or her. The photographer will not want a group picture, but two or a maximum of three people in action, rather than just talking. The actors should run the extract of the scene several times for the photographers. It is worth remembering that the photographers are looking for a good shot and are not so interested in the play itself, so they may well ask for the actors to make changes from the scene as rehearsed. The photos will take about half an hour. It is important to keep a good professional relationship with the photographers, because the same ones will very likely come to photograph publicity shots. You do not want to risk unflattering or comical images!

THE SECOND DRESS REHEARSAL

The next dress rehearsal should be the time when the actors are showing how the production will eventually feel. They ought to have had enough time onstage to make it their own, and the director can start to refine the production further. If it is going well, then many of the problems, which seemed hard to overcome at the first dress, will be solved – or at least appear less intrusive. During this dress the director should be able to decide if anything needs to be definitely changed. The rest of the creative team will be making their notes,

---

MAKING CUTS OR EDITS

- If the play is running too long, the first area for a cut is anything that, at the second dress rehearsal, seems superfluous to the narrative.
- In making any cuts, try not to penalize one individual too much. Even the most well-mannered actor will feel s/he has done something wrong if all the cuts fall on him/her.
- Do not be tempted, in the interests of fairness, to make a lot of little edits. This is the time to be bold and cut a whole page or whole section.
- While the actors affected by a large cut will probably be regretful of losing some lines or business, it will be far easier for them to learn the changed script, than a lot of little changes.
- In the end actors will be thankful to have a slimmed-down version, if it does not essentially change the dynamics of the piece.

---

and everyone should be looking at details: not the overarching, fundamental questions – these should all have been dealt with in the rehearsal room.

It is at this point that any final decisions about length and editing should be made. Typically, in the rehearsal room there will have been discussions and decisions about edits and changes, and it is likely very many will have been made. However, there is always something different about seeing the show onstage, and then later seeing it in front of an audience. As the director watches the second dress, s/he must be weighing up the value of each component.

After the second dress rehearsal, the timetable stays very much the same until the opening night. The director will have a notes' session and rehearse odd bits that need attention the morning after the second dress.

Depending on the scale of the production, there will either be one more dress that afternoon and then the opening that evening; or a series of previews leading to the opening night.

Opinions differ on what is the best routine for the day of the opening. The director who feels that the second of two performances in one day is always better, will want to have a dress rehearsal. Some directors feel the actors should conserve their energies and will just run sections of the play as a warm-up on the day of the first public performance. Directors will decide from experience their preferred way to run the day of the opening.

Having got to 5.00pm on the day of the opening (which is assumed to be at about 7.30pm or 8.00pm), the actors must be released to have a break, get something to eat and warm up. The director will probably want to have the cast together on stage at 6.30pm (for a 7.30pm start) to do a short warm-up or to run a couple of easy, good-humoured games and give a final, general note. The final note of 'Just enjoy it, I know I will' is too hackneyed to carry any weight, but at the other extreme an obscure, abstract note like, 'Just try and think purple as you each come on', is likely to cause derision. Think of something along the lines of, 'There's a full house tonight and they'll love all the hard work you've put in. It's really very funny/moving/thought provoking, and I'm sure will be terrific.'

The director ought to have bought and put into the dressing rooms a 'Best Wishes' card for each member of the cast, and a 'Thank You' card for the designer, choreographer, composer, lighting designer and DSM; and perhaps a card for teams of people like the rest of the stage management team, the stage crew, and the lighting and sound operators.

For the director, this is one of the most testing times of the whole production process – there is nothing left to do. The performance is in the hands of the cast and the technical crew. The traditional place for the director is in the bar with the producer or other management figures, possibly some board members and the incoming audience. Most directors prefer to watch the show standing at the back of the auditorium, the theory being they can make a quick escape, if necessary. The director should, however, overcome first-night anxiety and take notes as usual. The cast will not be grateful if, when they ask for notes, the director tells them s/he was too worried to take any.

A NOTE ON
AUDIENCE REACTION

After the transfer to the stage from the rehearsal room, which will have been very instructive in terms of what the play looks and sounds like, the next, and perhaps even more instructive, moment is putting the play in front of an audience. The director should be taking notes on the audience, as well as the actors. If the play is a comedy – are the audience laughing in the right places? It is worth remembering that the things that the cast found funny in the rehearsals will not necessarily be the same things the audience will laugh at. In fact many directors and actors are highly suspicious of 'rehearsal laughs' because so often what other actors find funny can be an in-joke that the audience cannot get.

Comedy is always more difficult to direct. If the audience do not hear every word, it is hard to get a joke. If the timing is not right, a joke might be lost. If the physicality of the performance is not right, the audience might not laugh. So the director at the first night checks that all of these ingredients are being given by the cast and being received by the audience. Is the build-up of the play – not too fast but not too sluggish – correctly contrived to get the spiralling-out-of-control effect that a Feydeau farce, a Dario Fo play or Frayn's *Noises Off* aims for? The director is aiming for laughs that cap each other, then a moment of recuperation for the audience. If it is funny, the director has won; if it is not funny, then the director, to some extent, has failed.

Drama or tragedy is easier because the audience can respond with many more shades of opinion. The audience will frequently be content with the play being quite moving or quite tragic.

AFTER THE
FIRST PERFORMANCE

At the end of the first performance, the director must immediately go backstage. S/he should straightaway find and thank the DSM, the stage crew, flymen and wardrobe. This is because the actors will be in the dressing rooms for at least a quarter of an hour, showering and getting changed, whereas the stage crew might well be leaving the building and heading for the local pub. Having thanked them, the director should go round the dressing rooms and – however the show has gone – present a positive face. The management or producer should provide some celebratory drinks, however modest. Usually the cast, the stage management and the wardrobe teams bond together, but although obviously invited, the stage and technical crew often find their own refreshment.

THE MORNING AFTER

The call for notes for the actors and stage management should be in the afternoon, allowing the morning to rest. If the play has gone well, the notes will be to tighten and improve bits and to pass on the audience's reactions as far as the director could identify them. If the play has not gone so well, the director needs to comfort the cast but avoid making wholesale, panic changes. The play has been rehearsed in all good faith. If the director has been even-handed, then ideas from the cast will have been incorporated and the whole enterprise should have the mark of a corporative undertaking. Everyone has a stake in it; it is not a good idea to try, in a limited time, to make great changes. Obviously, if there is the opportunity to identify particular improvements, they should be made. A bit of judicious editing; a change of pace; some slightly comic elements made more physical: all these sort of changes are useful, but the director must not undermine the confidence the cast have built up in the production by scything through the work that has been done. It is as well to remember that *Carmen*, one of the most popular operas in the world, was so savaged by the critics at its premiere that it is said to have led to Bizet's death.

The Reviews

The advice to any actor has to be: 'Don't ever read reviews'. No actor ever remembers the good bits of a review, only the bad ones. However, whatever the reviews, every actor in the cast will get a feeling of whether the reviews were good or not by the atmosphere in the audience and backstage. (I still carry with me the pain of a headline of a review that did not like my production of an adaptation of Kipling's *Jungle Book* – 'Beastly Bungle in the Jungle'!)

Smiling, pretty full houses, a bit of a buzz and it went OK. Small houses and grim faces backstage and it probably has not gone so well. The director should face up to the verdict of the critics and remind the cast that reviews are not read by many people, that good plays and performances generally transcend a bad review or two and that very many reviews are now written by people with no knowledge of theatre. Unfortunately, internet reviews are often worthless pieces of vindictive writing.

The best piece of advice for actors with regard to reviews (and, indeed, for everyone with regard to life) comes from the unlikely pen of Rudyard Kipling:

> If you can meet with Triumph and Disaster
> And treat those two impostors just the same
> . . . You'll be a Man, my son.

Forget the *Land of Hope and Glory* stuff – these are wise words, and well worth anyone in the theatre remembering. It is hurtful to get poor reviews, but every director should memorize a few entries from *No Turn Left Unstoned*, a book of reviews and critical comment compiled by Diana Rigg. It is very funny and surprising, and will put today's poor reviews in context. However, the director might learned something from reviews by long-term, reputable critics. One director's view of staging was changed by a review, and another always said he learnt the best lessons about Shakespeare direction from *The Guardian*.

Actors are generally a resilient lot and will have great loyalty to the production if a good, trusting relationship has been built up during the rehearsal period. If (or when) the show not going as well as hoped for, then the investment in taking care of the cast earlier yields dividends.

Keeping an Eye on the Production

The director might have another production to move on to after the first night but s/he must not abandon the production. The two complaints that actors have about directors after the show has opened are:

- The director is never seen again.
- The director is seen too often!

Having got the play on to the stage, the actors will very much want to make the play their own. The director must accept that to be the case; while it is entirely legitimate to give a few notes, the cast do not want to be called in for a full hour's worth of notes day after day. To be clear: if the show is in previews, then there will be notes and rehearsals; but once the press night has passed, the production becomes the actors' to refine as the audience leads them.

In the past, celebrity directors got a bad reputation by never being seen after the press night. Indeed, one cast of actors, at the Royal Shakespeare Company, reputedly sent a request to a TV company to see if it could arrange a meeting with their director because he had been so absent after the opening of the play. At the other end of the spectrum, John Barton (again at the RSC) insisted on giving notes after every performance, including the final performance – when, of course, the production would not be seen again. Both styles are guaranteed to annoy the cast. The director should come in to see the second and maybe third night; give some notes in the dressing rooms afterwards; and then let it go for a week. The important element the director has to control, as the play moves into its run, is the temptation for the actors to add unnecessary business and to become sloppy in their delivery of the text.

After a week, the director should watch a full performance and make notes to rein in any excesses and pick up details that have been lost. If new additions by the actors have been positive, then the director should thank the actors for them. However, the director should not be slow to remind the cast that the DSM sends him/her a show report every performance, which describes any changes the cast might make, and that the actor's duty is to ask the DSM to contact the director with new suggestions for the production the actor might want to instigate. The director will want to encourage developments, but in an orderly, regulated manner. The actors will appreciate this; they will not welcome an individual actor adding material to their scenes, possibly to the detriment of the scene and another actor's part, without the director's agreement.

THE LAST NIGHT

One of the satisfying aspects of being a stage director is the experience of being at the very beginning, at the inception of the production, and seeing it through to the end. The director should make every effort to attend the last night. It can be an emotional moment for the actors, and the director should want to be there to complete the circle. Actors often give each other last night presents but the director does not need to do so. Final night parties are feasible in London, as the majority of actors live in London. With productions in the regions, it is likely that actors will want to set off home after the last night, so the director should catch everyone immediately after the end of the performance for thanks and farewells.

The director should not hang about in the auditorium after the end of the show, because immediately the last performance ends, a gang of people will start clearing the stage and pulling down the set. Performance is ephemeral; that is one of its many attractions, but the brutal dismantling of the hardware is not an attractive last memory of a loved production.

9
DIRECTING OTHER TYPES OF PRODUCTION

The director will very often start his or her working career in the conventional stage situation, but most will find that over a career it is very common to branch out into many other areas. These will typically include opera, musicals, site-specific theatre, fringe theatre, children's theatre, corporate and theme park attractions, devised theatre, immersive and physical theatre, verbatim theatre and probably other forms too. New ideas are emerging all the time and the director needs to keep abreast of innovatory trends. Where possible use the new ideas from one area to fertilize other, perhaps more traditional, forms of theatre.

OPERA

There are two major differences for the theatre director to take on board when working on an opera. The first, *huge* difference between the familiar, straight, spoken-text theatre production and opera is that the overriding priority for the opera singers is the music. This might sound obvious, but it has all sorts of ramifications. The second difference is that the director is not in charge. The ultimate authority in opera is the music director or the conductor – usually the same person.

OPPOSITE: *The Battle of Quiberon Bay.* Beautiful models of man-of-war ships, with working cannons, recreated the sea battle of the Napoleonic War. It was enacted in the Roman Baths as part of the Bath Festival to the music of Handel with new words, sung by Britannia and France's Marianne. ARNIM FREISS

Opera Auditions

Casting a singer is in some ways more cut-and-dried than casting actors in straight plays. Singers know their range and will know what roles their voice makes them right to be cast in. Actors, by comparison, can be cast according to type or adventurously cast against type. In auditioning for an opera, no attention will paid, in the first instance, to acting. The primary point of an opera audition is to hear the singer's voice. The director and musical director will already know the singer will be technically suitable for the role, because he or she would not be auditioning for a role out of their vocal range. If it's agreed by the musical director that the auditionee's voice has the right sound, then a discussion can be held with the director about the physical suitability of the person for the role. It is worth mentioning that while actors will come to an audition in casual clothing and ready to improvise or move if asked, the singers will often come dressed formally, ready to sing, but not to do anything else. Once it has been decided who are the eligible singers, this smaller group might be called back and the director could instigate some very straightforward exercises to try out their acting skills, but even this is not routine. There is no point, of course, asking the singer to read anything because they will be singing in all but a very few operas where there are some interspersed spoken passages, like *The Magic Flute* and *Carmen*. However, if there are some spoken passages, the director must hear the candidate. Very often there is a huge difference between a singer's singing voice and their onstage speaking voice – it is often surprisingly soft.

Opera Rehearsals

Once a singer has been cast, s/he will learn the part before rehearsals begin. Because the opera repertoire is very much smaller than that of the theatre, the singer is very likely to be familiar with the part or perhaps has sung the role before. The first day of an opera rehearsal is a very nice surprise for directors of straight drama. The singers arrive knowing their music, so the sing through (equivalent of the read through) usually sounds like the finished article.

The director and designer will introduce the production in the conventional way, before the sing through. After the sing through, the cast will have questions and a discussion with the conductor/ musical director. They will be interested in the production ideas of the director but in a different way from actors. Actors will want to immerse themselves in the world of the play (sometimes going to extremes to do so), whereas singers will readily go along with the ideas of the director, but in a slightly detached way. For the actor, the whole world of the production matters and affects their performance; for the singer, the music is the priority. One of the results is that singers are often easier to direct. The singer sees the rehearsal process divided between music rehearsals and staging rehearsals, not as a single entity. If this sounds as if it makes life difficult, nothing is further from the truth. Singers in opera are very willing to commit themselves to whatever the director asks.

Perhaps it is because there has been a tradition of wild opera productions – or maybe because it is

Scene from *Sweeney Agonistes*, a powerful, short, music theatre piece with music by Stephen McNeff. RICHARD WILLIAMS

a completely artificial medium – that questions of naturalism (which actors punish themselves with trying to define and achieve) are very absent from opera rehearsals. Singers will sometimes check on the why and wherefore of their character's actions, but will much happier to do things that many actors would find difficult to justify. This can be exhilarating. It has led to very many exciting productions.

Listen to the Music

The novice opera director needs to very aware of the music itself. The music already has within it a shape and an emotion. It is very important that the director follows the intrinsic shape of the music. Where the composer has written a very bright, vigorous aria (a solo piece of singing), it would be working against the musical imperative to decide to make the action sluggish and dull. In *Carmen*, for example, it is very hard to ignore the seductive tones of *The Habanera* or the excitement of the start of the last act outside the bullring. So the staging needs, usually, to be appropriate to the music, although occasionally a particular effect might be achieved by running against it. The music also has a fixed length, so the staging has to fit its length. This is not to say the director has to find frantic action for every moment, but the overall staging must be in sympathy in style and length with the music. This means that the director will probably spend time preparing their staging and the timing of it, with the music in more detail than the dramatic, acting equivalent.

Once in rehearsal, the director will be expected to work at a faster pace than for a play. It is accepted that the director will have a detailed plan worked out in advance. The training for opera singers does not concentrate on teaching detailed acting techniques. Because the music carries a lot of the narrative and emotional content, there is less need for the singer to carry those responsibilities. Again, one result of this is that the singer, generally speaking, has a much less possessive attitude towards the character than in straight plays.

Opera singers today are often expected to work within very extravagant staging, as anyone who attends opera regularly knows. The singers will do it willingly, so long as their singing is not compromised. So, for example, singers at The English National Opera found themselves singing all over a set that was a vast, reclining, naked woman in Ligeti's *Le Grand Macabre*. Designers and directors have worked very hard over the past twenty years or more to breathe new life into old operas, and the singers have taken it all on the chin. This is the excitement for the director brought up on the naturalism that dictates the look and feel of so much theatre, and all film and television drama. In opera there is more possibility of surrealism, of dream and of extravagant imagination.

Any staging the director wants to invent is possible, so long as the singer is in a good physical position when he or she has to sing. As with all performance, downstage centre and facing the audience is the prime position. Although singers will not gravitate there automatically, they do want a good place onstage, whether standing or moving. It is very important for the conductor and the singer to have eye contact. This can be either direct, live contact or via TV screens placed strategically on the set or in the wings. The director should be aware that the singer's sound tends to disappear upwards when the singer is behind the proscenium arch, so keep bringing the scenes downstage.

Another consideration in directing opera is that the singers are exerting their voices and cannot be expected to sing out in the way an actor could speak out for a full day's rehearsal. Singers will very often 'sing under' or speak their part in rehearsal if they feel their voice is getting tired.

Rehearsing an opera scene will begin with the cast singing through the scene or section to be rehearsed. A pianist (*repetiteur*) plays for rehearsals. The singers check musical details with the conductor before the director takes over for a staging rehearsal. All will be well so long as the director has fully understood the needs of the singers, as outlined above.

The Three Ladies from *The Magic Flute* at the Bath International Music Festival. Many operas today are produced in modern dress, often with spectacular results. Opera is, by its nature, non-naturalistic and so surreal and imaginative interpretations are very common. MIKE EDDOWS

Double-Casting

Many opera companies double-cast the principal roles; that is, two singers are cast in the same role. This must be factored into the rehearsal schedule and does not normally cause problems in the way it might with a play. Actors are going through the process of creating the characters for themselves and using the techniques outlined earlier in the book. Thus the creation of the character is highly personalized. Because singers do not have the same priority, double-casting works without difficulty.

If it seems that opera singers don't care about the acting side of performance, it is necessary to give reassurance that nothing is further from the truth. The opera singer will want to give their performance clarity of characterization, truthful emotion and recognizable relationships. It is just that their training is rarely about Stanislavski; they have the enormous responsibility of getting the music right and they do not have the same possessiveness over making the part uniquely theirs. They are aware of the history of great singers before them, in these roles, and want to rise to the musical and technical challenge of the music.

Rehearsals continue along these lines, gradually working on larger and larger sections of the opera until the last few days. Towards the end of the time in the rehearsal room – or at the start of time onstage – the orchestra will arrive for the *Sitzprobe*. This rehearsal brings together the cast and the orchestra for the first time, and it is the session in which the singers can hear what the orchestra will be playing and any problems can be sorted out. The orchestral texture will be different from rehearsals with the piano, so this is a crucial moment for the cast and director.

Lighting

Because of the prevailing theatre tradition of naturalism, there is a significant difference in plotting the lighting for opera. The opera lighting designer will use a follow spot to illuminate the singers. This means that the lighting design for the general view of the set can be very much more 'painterly' than is usually the case in straight theatre. This might not be the case in smaller opera companies (of which there are an increasing number, doing very high-quality work around the country).

Stage and Piano Rehearsals

After the *Sitzprobe*, the cast will start the tech on-stage, much in the same way as for a play. Until the dress rehearsal, the technical and other rehearsals of parts of scenes will be described as 'stage and piano'. The conductor will be working

with the orchestra until both parties come together in what is called the general rehearsal, which is the same as a dress rehearsal in the theatre.

Another difference between rehearsing an opera and a play is the routine on the day of the first performance. Singers must rest their voices, so there will not be a dress rehearsal. There might be a rehearsal where the principal roles are double-cast, and this is an opportunity for the second cast to get on stage and rehearse. However, the director should assume that there will not be a rehearsal, other than an emergency walk through, with piano, of some scenes that need attention.

There is one other convention that the director should be aware of: at the end of the press night performance, the conductor, director and designer will be invited by the cast to come and take a bow onstage with the cast.

MUSICALS

Pre-Rehearsals

The role of the director in a musical is to collaborate with the musical director, the composer and the choreographer. Unlike opera, the director is the

IMPORTANT NOTES ON DIRECTING AN OPERA FOR THE FIRST TIME

Many directors of opera come from straight theatre. Here are some vital tips:
* Spend a lot of time listening to the music in preparation for rehearsals.
* Be prepared, especially in Baroque opera, for repetitions. If the director is not musically trained, s/he needs to get someone to translate the musical instructions and explain the two dots like a colon (:) indicating a repetition of the first part of the aria. This repetition is called the *da capo*, meaning 'from the top'.
* The opera score will often be written in a foreign language and the production more often than not will be sung in it (usually German, Italian, Russian or French). The director needs to get a translation, which can come from a CD booklet, and write in the translation, using pencil.
* Use pencil because the scores will be hired (at some expense) and will be collected at the end of the run and sent back to the music publishers.
* Understand that the cast of the opera will know the opera in detail and in a way that actors do not know plays.
* Take advantage of the freedom that opera offers in terms of exciting and innovative ideas about staging.
* Never forget that the singers must be in a good place both to sing to the audience and to see the conductor.

final arbiter of the production. That said, because of the nature of musicals, the three creative directors must work in very close connection with each other. In practice this means those three sitting down and doing very careful preparations with the designer. Naturally, the choreographer will generally want flat, open spaces for the dance numbers, which will influence the design.

Like operas, musicals are usually built round a group of principal characters, who sing solos, duets, trios and even quartets, and the chorus, who will provide the musical weight for the exciting, big numbers. Every number will be choreographed. Singers in musicals may not have the same training in sight-reading music as opera singers, but will frequently learn their songs from the time dedicated to note-bashing at the piano in rehearsal. A lot of time, maybe a quarter to a third of the rehearsal period, must be allowed for piano rehearsals when scheduling.

Auditions

In opera the singers do not necessarily need to dance; whereas in musicals, performers will only be cast because they are excellent at the so called 'triple threat' – singing, dancing and acting. The auditions for a musical will often start with dancing, followed by singing and finally acting. (This will depend to some extent on the type of show, of course.) Although all elements of the 'triple threat' are considered equally important, good acting cannot cover any weakness in song and dance. The process will differ for ensemble (chorus) and principals. The ensemble will often be a mixture of performers who can sing better than they can dance, and vice versa. Some ensemble members will also be cast as understudies to the principals. Auditions for West End shows can be very exhaustive. With long runs and with high costs (*Spiderman the Musical* cost $60 million; approximately £45 million in 2017 prices) and expectations, the producers need to be absolutely certain of the strength of the casting all the way through the roles. Elaine Paige went through eight rounds of auditions for *Evita*.

The stage director cannot rehearse the show until the cast is well advanced with the individual songs and dances. In a typical musical, 50 per cent of the stage time is sung and danced, and some – like *The Phantom of the Opera* – are sung through, like an opera. The schedule will, therefore, prioritize the musical elements for the first ten days or two weeks. Cast members will record their music as an aid to learning. As the cast become confident with singing the numbers, the choreographer will start to introduce dance elements; after about two weeks, the songs are pretty much fixed and the basics of the choreography are in place. With the musical numbers learnt both musically and choreographically, the director will then start working on the scenes, particularly with the principals.

Rehearsals

One theatre director who had moved into working on musicals said he preferred directing them because he only had to be responsible for a third of the final product! There is some truth in this, but the buck finally stops with the director. The director will find there is less room to manoeuvre in a musical than a straight play. The cast's interest in Stanislavski and all that represents will be somewhere between the actors in a play and the cast of an opera, but probably more in sympathy with the priorities of the opera singers. The director's job is to get very high-definition performances out of the actors to match the high emotion and energy generated by the music. However, the acting must not shrink into two-dimensional melodrama just because of the force nine gale of music. This is not an easy balance to achieve, and so a director new to musicals would be advised to watch, live or on film, as much of the genre as possible. Start by looking at the older traditional Broadway hit musicals like *Oklahoma* and *Calamity Jane*, then move on to *Sweet Charity* and the work of Stephen Sondheim.

Technical and Dress Rehearsals

Even in a small cast musical like *Sweeney Todd*, the tech will take a lot of time because of the complexity of movement and dancing on the set, audibility and radio mics, and the number of people involved, both onstage and in the production team. The mics give great flexibility, but using them throws a great responsibility on getting the right equipment and a skilled sound engineer to mix the band and the vocals, all of which are amplified. The director should triple the tech time s/he would expect for a play. The technical rehearsal will be with piano and drums, and the full orchestra or band will join for the dress rehearsals. The performers will expect to work on the day of the first performance, either doing extracts or even a dress rehearsal. It is noticeable that – because of the unremitting schedule of rehearsal and performances – singers in musicals have more problems with their voices than opera singers. This is why there are frequent stories of members of the ensemble (chorus) getting an unexpected break and hitting the headlines with their success as an understudy taking over a starring role.

In planning a musical, or even a show with music, the director ought to be aware of the growing number of successful productions using actor/musicians – actors who play instruments to a professional level. *Sweeney Todd* and *Sunset Boulevard* have both been West End hits using actor/musicians.

Musicals and operas seem to suffer the same fate: there are so many variables in the production that they tend to be either hits or flops! Even the magical Cameron Mackintosh had a failure with *Moby Dick – the Musical*. Good luck!

PRODUCTIONS FOR CHILDREN

The UK has a poor record in providing theatre for children. Since the Harry Potter phenomenon, however, it has been widely understood that the children's market can offer financial returns, and there is an increased interest in children's theatre. In the UK, the leading building-based companies are The Unicorn and Polka Theatre in London, and The Egg in Bath, part of The Theatre Royal. There are very many children's touring theatre companies spread throughout the country. Some specialize in visiting schools and others tour to theatres where the children's audience travel to the venue in groups, as arranged by parents or schools.

The best advice given to a director when starting to work in children's theatre was: 'Remember this is not just the first time the children will see theatre, it is likely to be the *only* time they will see theatre – so make it good!'.

Adult audiences are very forgiving – they understand the convention that they are supposed to suspend their disbelief. So, for example, if a piece of masking is missing and the audience sees the actors waiting to come on, the audience sees it and dismisses it. The adults know that part of the unspoken contract is to overlook discrepancies like that. An adult audience will be very willing, almost primed, to laugh at a comedy. Even if something is only half funny, or not even half, an audience will do its best to be encouraging. All of this is as it should be. But it is not the case with a children's audience.

A children's audience will simply believe what it sees. This makes the director's job more exacting, not easier. It is a mistake to trade on the apparent ease with which children will enter an imaginary world and give them less than the very best.

Ambitious Plays for a Young Audience

Although children's theatre is taken more and more seriously, it still remains a starting point for actors and directors, rather than a destination. Taking that situation as a given for the time being, the director can help to make the sector more generally appealing, while giving the audience an experience that satisfies and extends the audience's imaginations. The Unicorn Theatre has produced slim versions of Shakespeare, Brecht plays and even a Mozart opera to great critical acclaim and to immense audience appreciation. In considering productions for a young audience, the director should aim high in every respect. The themes should be challenging; the designs, music, choreography and direction should be at the highest level. No part of the thinking behind a children's production should include the idea that, 'It's only kids. It's easy.' The thinking ought to be: 'It's young people – that's a real challenge to get it right.'

Performance for Children

Children are used to not understanding every word in every sentence. They grow up making as much sense of words as they can by listening to the tone of the speaker and reacting to the context of the speech. While it will be helpful to avoid very specific vocabulary, it is a mistake to go for the lowest common denominator in spoken English,

just because the listeners are young. Seven, eight and nine year-olds can readily come to grips with a Shakespeare play that is vigorously performed – just like the adult version should be too! An adjustment will have to be made in the length of time the young audience is asked to sit still without visiting the loo. For a young person, forty-five minutes is long enough without a break (and adult audiences too, often!). If the young audience is bored, the children will want to go much earlier and more frequently.

Inexperienced directors of children's productions can become worried if their audience is talking. But there are two types of talking. First, is the bored, restless, uninterested talk that is not whispered and is accompanied by twisting and turning in the seats. This has to be remedied by making alterations to the performance. The other type is the child whispering to a fellow school pupil or younger brother or sister, while keeping a focus on the stage – this is a question being answered about the play. It is constructive, not destructive, and should not cause any worries.

The Wizard of Oz – one of the perennially popular family shows at the Haymarket Theatre, Basingstoke. ARNIM FREISS

GETTING STARTED IN YOUNG PEOPLE'S THEATRE

- Learn about the activities of theatre for young people by looking at the Theatre for Young Audiences' (TYA) website and join the organization.
- TYA is the UK branch of ASSITEJ, which is the International Association of Theatre for Young People (the acronym stands for the French wording).
- Go and see the work of companies like Company of Angels, M6, Pilot, Bone Ensemble, Oily Carte, Action Transport or Kazzum.
- Remember that young people have a strong feeling about justice. How can that theme be translated into a stage play?
- Get to know an existing children's or young persons' theatre company and suggest ideas to them.

The director, working with professional actors, does not need to dumb-down the production. The best standpoint to take is remembering the audience will contain adults who have brought the children – either family or teachers. If, in the show, there is something that the adult will think is 'just for the kiddies', then it ought to be rethought. This is not to say that the director ought to be looking at staging Dostoyevsky for nine-year-olds, but long-lasting commercial shows like *The Lion King* (based on *Hamlet* and directed by the great American director Julie Taymor) show that sophistication is never wasted on the young.

Although it has been a neglected sector in the UK – especially compared to some Eastern European countries where theatre for children is well established, properly funded and plays an important and recognized part of cultural life – it is an area where a director can make a significant impact.

FRINGE SHOWS

Since the explosion of The Fringe at the Edinburgh Festival everyone knows what a fringe show is. It predominantly involves young directors and actors working to a short time-slot in a busy venue, financing the project themselves, often from a school or youth theatre, having a great time – and occasionally putting on a wonderful hit show. The show will usually be simple from the technical point of view, often consists of a small cast and will champion new writing over older, well-established writers.

The main problems the director will come across when putting together a fringe show are the lack of resources and the wavering commitment of the cast as they juggle their paid work commitments with rehearsals.

A director can sometimes get involved with some sort of off-the-wall production. The director gets drawn in either because:

- It sounded like a good idea at the time (possibly after a few drinks!).
- Because personal finances were low and it did not seem to be a disastrous idea.
- For some other reason.

It is not easy to predict how these will work out. Sometimes a group of near amateurs can get an idea that happens to take off. *Night Collar* was a series of sketches about being a cabbie in Liverpool. Broad humour, combined with a mixed cast of a couple of known local actors and some amateurs, produced a hit that played to capacity houses. A big success at the time of writing is *The Play That Goes Wrong*, written and produced by a group of drama students.

Because there are so few guarantees in the theatre business, it is always worth taking a punt on an apparently crazy idea. There may be no money at the start but amazing things can happen – and do!

SITE-SPECIFIC THEATRE

The idea of producing a piece of drama in a non-purpose-built venue is not new. The medieval mystery plays were performed on the streets, on and around a four-wheeled wagon. In the latter part of the twentieth century, the idea of performing a piece of theatre connected to the place where it was being performed, grew in popularity. Over the past thirty years the description 'site-specific' has broadened its meaning to include almost anything that is performed in a non-theatre venue, losing the earlier sense of linking the performance to the place and its history.

The cellars of Shoreditch Town Hall for performances of short Pinter plays about fascist regimes certainly gave an appropriately oppressive and dangerous atmosphere. The same is true of the various venues used by Theatre Delicatessen for its plays about modern Britain, performed in vacant offices and warehouses.

There are two linked considerations for the director. Does the location add a real *frisson* to the performance? If so, is it enough of a *frisson* to justify the trouble and expense of making the venue into a

sort of theatre, for that is now the expectation? Theatre companies hang lights in woods for *A Midsummer Night's Dream* and import sound equipment into disused abattoirs for *Medea*. The risks are high – the audience stands, portable toilets have to be hired, the weather can change at any moment – but the rewards, if it all goes well, are enormous. An audience has had a never-to-be-repeated experience. Find an interesting place, link the story to it, work out a budget and start fundraising.

IMMERSIVE THEATRE

Immersive theatre is a close relative of site-specific theatre. Both genres also include possible promenade performances. The stage director must acknowledge that immersive theatre is as much an

The set for *The Chalk Legend*, a large-scale music theatre project performed at the National Sailing Centre, Weymouth, as part of the Cultural Olympiade. A local story of Vikings and Saxons, produced by the Bournemouth Symphony Orchestra with music by Stephen McNeff. BOURNEMOUTH SYMPHONY ORCHESTRA

A FEW THOUGHTS ON SITE-SPECIFIC PERFORMANCES

- It is best to link the content of the show to the location, not just use a space for a play that could happen anywhere else.
- If the venue and the content of the play connect, then the space can do all the work a set would do in a conventional stage show.
- Just as a conventional stage show creates a convincing metaphorical world that has its own consistency, conventions and aesthetic, it is the same with a site-specific show.
- The audience's focus can more easily be lost, so it needs very sharp, high-definition acting.
- Outdoor performances risk losing audibility, especially if the space is too large.
- It is useful to think how much of the story can be told with movement, as well as spoken word.

art event as a theatre event. The audience follows the action from place to place, or room to room. Each space is created with great emphasis being placed on the detail of props, costumes, sound and lighting effects, much as it might be stepping on to a film set. The audience might follow a set sequence of the action or follow a particular actor. The overall effect is of a collage of impressions. Immersive theatre is in one sense the ultimate Stanislavski performance. The director, when rehearsing the actors, is duty bound to drill them on their 'given circumstances' and every other aspect of the Stanislavski system. The actors live the role more closely than in a normal theatre set-up.

The timescale and rehearsal demands are very varied. The brand leader in the UK at the moment is Punchdrunk.

DEVISED THEATRE

The stage director is very likely to be involved at some point with devised theatre. It is a very popular form, especially among youth theatre groups, educational units attached to theatres, colleges and universities and senior citizens' groups. For the director this can be both a triumph and a challenge: the democratic nature of the project can be appealing, but there are always moments of disagreement and some measure of despair.

The director must start with a passion for the subject matter. Many devised plays centre on a social problem or question, something that the group can feel energized by over a lengthy and often difficult rehearsal period.

The first step is to fill the rehearsal room and the participants' minds with the bedrock of the project – researched material. The cast should be divided into pairs and sent off with a specific topic to research. In the preface to the published play, Victor Spinetti gives a good account of the process Joan Littlewood adopted to create the masterpiece *Oh, What a Lovely War*, and there is plenty of information available at the websites of any of the companies given in the Box. One element of the success of *Lovely War* was that Littlewood was in charge. While the democratic process can be great for researching and creating a pool of ideas, theatre

FIVE RULES WHEN STARTING A DEVISED THEATRE PROJECT

- For a successful collaboration, the number of people involved in the project, or central creative part of it, should not be more than seven.
- The group should agree how it is going to work together. A set of rules – agreed by everyone – should be displayed in the rehearsal room.
- Study at the work of the best devising companies, e.g. Complicité, Frantic Assembly, Improbable, Kneehigh and Filter. Attend one of their workshops, if possible.
- The dynamics of creativity are very clearly exposed in devised work. The group must understand that all creativity starts with huge enthusiasm, inevitably dips in the middle and rises towards the end of the time allocated. Don't be depressed or surprised by the dip.
- Make a realistic timetable, with a first performance date – and stick to it.

is not essentially a democratic set-up. A director whose aesthetic will determine the final shape, look and sound of the devised piece is needed.

Once the director has collated the research, the cast, perhaps in pairs, should turn their research into a dramatized presentation. This is then shown to the rest of the group. This is the basic material. What the director should be looking for is a personal story or stories on which to hang the main event. For example, in a devised play about the thalidomide tragedy entitled *The Apple of Our Eye*, the figure of David Mason, the main campaigner for the children's rights, emerged as a pivotal figure and he became the protagonist. In *Lovely War* it is the common soldier who is the hero and he should be evident even in the scenes between the officers.

Timescale

A devised play emerges slowly; this is where the director has to adopt a pastoral, as well as a directorial, role, keeping the group from becoming impatient. With a possible storyboard worked out, the cast is given characters to play and different parts of the narrative, which they must again research. Then the improvisation of the scenes can start. The improvisations must be recorded, so that valuable material is not lost. The director has to set up the improvisations so that the relevant material is used and the focus on characterization is not lost. It is important to make clear to the cast that a devised play is not the same as a verbatim or documentary play. Often the language of a devised play can be flat, lacking in colour and poetry. This is a mistake – listen to the way people express themselves in everyday life: it is frequently quaint, curious and refreshing. Some companies bring in a writer at this point to write up the material with an outsider's perspective and give it a different, perhaps more poetic, tone.

Mike Leigh's style of devising plays is through character creation first, slowly adding a narrative. It has produced some highly acclaimed work like *Abigail's Party*, but the process is slow. However,

it does point to another possibility, which is to bring in a writer once the research and improvised scenes have been completed. The advantage of this is that an outside eye at the later stages of the process can often bring a stronger dramatic arc to the finished play; the outsider is free from the biases of the participants in devising.

VERBATIM THEATRE

This form of theatre falls into two categories. In one, the director and the cast research the subject and together devise the play. It differs from devised theatre because everything spoken on stage is a *verbatim reconstruction*. That is to say, every word onstage has been recorded from a living person. In the second version, the script is sourced from records of events, and shaped and edited by the writer. In this case, the director's job is more or less that of directing a conventional play, as the rehearsals will begin with a script.

Origins

Peter Cheeseman at the Victoria Theatre in Stoke-on-Trent pioneered the former version of verbatim theatre in the 1970s. Among his great successes was *The Fight for Shelton Bar*, which traced the attempt by steel workers to stop the closure of the local works. The cast and the director researched the material by talking to the people concerned and turning it into a dynamic story. Each performance culminated in an appearance by some of the actual people involved. Like Littlewood, Cheeseman took editorial control to shape the story into a dramatic form.

Among the most acclaimed of the second style of verbatim plays are the Tribunal Plays, staged by Nick Kent at London's Tricycle Theatre. In his version of verbatim theatre, the written record of tribunals, reports and government investigations were shaped into a dramatic form with outstanding successes like *The Colour of Justice* – a reconstruction of The Stephen Lawrence Inquiry – and *Guantanamo: Honor Bound to Defend Freedom*, written by Victoria Brittain and Gillian Slovo from spoken evidence.

Verbatim is a form of theatre that lends itself to contemporary themes and the reconstruction of adversarial situations, like trials and political debates. For the director it is a chance to make a mark by grabbing an up-to-the-minute issue and making a contribution to a live debate.

PHYSICAL THEATRE

If a director has strong dance, martial arts', gymnastics' or sports' interests/ability, then physical theatre should be an area to investigate. There are a number of circus and physical theatre courses, which – although primarily intended for performers – provide a great jumping-off point for someone with ambitions to direct in this area. Perhaps the best-known director to come from physical theatre training is Simon McBurney, who trained at the Le Coq School in Paris. His company, Theatre de Complicité, started with a strong emphasis on physical comedy, winning the Perrier Award for comedy at The Edinburgh Fringe in 1983. The work of the company is underpinned by its original principles: an emphasis on visual, physical, devised theatre, which is strong on narrative, often taking a surreal turn. In recent times, McBurney has increasingly used technology, video and computer art in the company's work.

Any young director today would be well advised to develop their visual imagination. If past developments are any guide to the future, the direction of travel of theatre over the past twenty-five years has been away from *text* and text interpretation towards theatre that is devised, visual, physical and musical. Contemporary physical theatre is cross-disciplinary and often includes use of puppetry, for example. The young director can expand their visual awareness by seeing the work of performers and companies, and/or taking a place on a workshop or course, from the artist and companies listed below:

- Stephen Berkoff
- Pina Bausch
- James Thiérreé
- Chickenshed
- Complicité
- DV8
- Gecko
- Horse and Bamboo Theatre
- Kneehigh Theatre
- Spymonkey
- Trestle Theatre
- Circomedia (Bristol, England)
- East 15 BA Physical Theatre (London)
- National Centre for Circus Arts (London)
- L'Ecole Jacques Lecoq (France)
- Headlong Performance Institute (USA)
- Pig Iron for Advanced Training (USA)

Physical theatre is almost exclusively created through devising. The director, as always with devising, needs to keep a very clear view of the objectives, while allowing enough freedom for creative invention.

OTHER POSSIBLE PLACES IN WHICH A DIRECTOR MIGHT WORK

Adaptations

A director will almost certainly find him/herself writing at some point. Very often it will be an adaptation of a well-known title – a book, a film or even a poem. The reasons can be that it is cheaper to do-it-yourself; or because the requirements of the production, in terms of casting and doubling, are too specific to hand over to a commissioned writer. Whatever the reason, the director directing his or her own work must be as open to comment from the cast in rehearsal as when a printed script from any other source is being prepared. It is rather embarrassing for all concerned if the director has adapted a novel but cannot find any fault with his or her own work. Adaptation is a pleasurable job; in many ways it requires the director to imaginatively plan the production and to build it into a script.

Puppets

There is an increased use of puppets in contemporary theatre. Until recently, puppets were thought of as an entertainment for children only. While it is certain that the serious use of puppets had already started, it was The National Theatre's production of *Warhorse* that finally announced their arrival as a legitimate part of the director's repertoire. Puppets can come in many different forms, such as the visibly manipulated Bunraku from Japan, shadow puppets, arm puppets, table puppets and so on. Mixing live action with puppets can be extremely effective, and can produce both moving and comic results. For example, the use of a puppet, playing the part of a child, in Anthony Minghella's *Madame Butterfly* at the English National Opera was hailed with rapturous approval for its highly emotional effect, and the Certain Dark Things company had a hit with *Melancholy*. At the other end of the scale, Pants on Fire company's *Fumidor* and *Metamorphosis* made hilarious comic use of puppets.

Shadow puppets and the use of shadows generally can be a highly atmospheric addition to a production. This particular use of puppetry does not need expert help but generous time allocated to using shadows of objects; cut-outs on a sheet can be very rewarding.

The director using other types of puppetry will generally need to take advice from an experienced puppeteer to gain most from their use.

THEME PARKS

With a growth in the commercial theme park business there is more work for the stage director in this situation. In general, the budgets will be generous because the entertainment will be expected to last for a year or more. The shows in this context are characterized by being loud, very visual, light on text, comic or scary, with an adventure narrative and short. The length will only be ten to fifteen minutes because the audience is expected to move around to other attractions.

For the director it can be both lucrative and testing. S/he will have to distil all ideas into a very concentrated, simple narrative, and will have to produce work that is very entertaining for a wide age range of children, offering something to the adults as well. It is above all expected to be fun. In this respect it has some similarities to the traditional British pantomime. The essential quality is directness and clarity. This is not a place for complexity or subtlety.

WORKING OVERSEAS

If a director is invited to work overseas, grab the offer with both hands. The chance to experience – first-hand – the discipline of actors from another culture and audiences from another country should never be passed over. As a general rule, a director must be flexible and able to respond to changing circumstances; things might well change day by day. A basic need might be a good translator – and don't assume someone else will have thought of that. The writer arrived in Indonesia to direct a play only to discover the organizers had forgotten about a translator! It will also need a lot more rehearsal time than expected in the UK; think about doubling the time. And be prepared to learn some very different ways of thinking about theatre, especially in a non-European context. When I went to Indonesia to direct a play, The British Council sent me out six months in advance to meet the actors and to decide on what play to do. I told the Indonesian cast that because of the need to translate everything, they should look at and learn the play before I got back. I returned home and six months later started to rehearse in Jakarta. A few days into the rehearsal the lead actor was away. I asked for one of the other cast members to read in, but he knew the part anyway. For the next scene I chose a different actor to read in and he too knew the part. Very surprised, I asked how they all knew the other parts. 'You told

Shadow puppets from a production of the opera *Háry János* at the Dartington International Festival. Very simple but rather beautiful, the shadow puppets can change size and do all kinds of cinematic tricks. RICHARD WILLIAMS

us to learn the play, so we have done.' The whole cast knew the whole play! That's commitment!

MASKS AND COMMEDIA DELL'ARTE

The stage director should understand the possibilities of masks and of Commedia. From the heroes of Ancient Greek theatre through to the devil in the medieval mystery plays, from Commedia dell'Arte to modern theatre-makers like Dario Fo and Peter Brook, the mask has a magical or supernatural quality. It has been said of the mask that it 'comes alive without pretending to be alive'. Although not widely used in contemporary theatre, where naturalism rules the roost, it crops up in unlikely places; for example, Nina Conte's ventriloquism act, Brecht's *Mann ist Mann* and in Julie Taymor's production of Stravinsky's *Oedipus Rex*. The history and the multiple uses of the mask, together with the philosophy that surrounds it, make it an area that any director should investigate. It is very easy to find evening, weekend and summer courses dedicated to teaching mask work.

The same is true for Commedia dell'Arte. The traditional, outdoor comedy of stereotypes and stereotypical situations, originating in Renaissance Italy, comes to us today in the silent films of the early twentieth century and most television situation comedies. Again, it is very easy to find a course or an expert from whom to learn about this important genre. Both masks and Commedia should be as much in the director's bag of tricks as skilful techniques, such as actioning and improvisation.

The great attraction of working in the arts in general – and the theatre in particular – is the enormously wide range of methods to employ when working, and the huge range of places and types of work a director might be involved in. These are among the reasons why people choose stage directing over regular office work!

10
TOURING, REVIVALS AND REPLACEMENT REHEARSALS

TOURING

A Changing Ecology

With the decline in the regional repertory system there has been an increased interest in touring theatre around the UK. Touring is divided into categories according to the size of the theatres. A number one tour would visit the larger theatres, such as: The Apollo, Oxford; The Theatre Royal Brighton; The Grand, Blackpool; The Alhambra, Bradford; and Hippodrome, Bristol. These theatres are usually Victorian or Edwardian and generally have a seating capacity of over a thousand seats. A middle-scale tour would visit theatres, such as: The Playhouse, Oxford; The Arts Theatre, Cambridge; and The Theatre Royal, Bury St Edmunds. These are theatres with about five-hundred seats. Small-scale theatres seat an audience of about two-hundred in theatres like The Lawrence Batley in Huddersfield or The Unity in Liverpool.

With the shift in funding policy from The Arts Council, and with the theatres themselves finding it hard to support a full-time company, most regional theatres are now a hybrid of some self-produced work, some touring product and some non-straight theatre, which can include stand-up comedy, cinema relays of plays and operas, and screenings of films.

OPPOSITE: Mark Rylance in *Airbase* at the Arts Theatre, London. A story about American airmen based in the UK. It was so controversial that questions were asked about it in Parliament. ALISTAIR MUIR

The result is that there are many small companies, as well as larger ones, on the road, visiting both established touring circuits and a more random selection of rep theatres. The touring productions from larger commercial companies are commonly a West End play, either before or after its West End run, or a revival of an old West End hit with a star name in it; sometimes a new play, supported by a star cast. The larger theatres need the big names or a sure-fire title to get the audience in. A typical touring product might be something like *The Importance of Being Earnest* with Nigel Havers and Martin Jarvis, or *The Lion, the Witch and The Wardrobe* with a cast of unknown – but classy – actors. Smaller scale tours tend to present more adventurous subjects. Whatever the scale of the tour, the director faces the same challenges in each case.

Rehearsals, Tech and Opening

Rehearsals would take the normal shape, whatever is the preferred method of the director. At the end of rehearsals, the cast will move to the first theatre on the tour. The producer will have previously made arrangements for the stage, lighting and flying crews to be on hand for the opening of the new show. The producer will also have arranged for wardrobe staff to travel to the venue. The producer and the venue will want the show to open as soon as possible, so box office money can be taken. The director is, therefore, under pressure to work fast on the lighting, the tech and the dress rehearsals. More or less time will be designated to

get the show on stage, depending on the scale of it. The director is almost certainly going to have to work with a group of people s/he has not worked with before, and under strong pressure to work at top speed. The crew will be unfamiliar with the show, which can also cause problems.

It is here that ultra-careful preparation with the designer and lighting designer, months earlier, will bring dividends. It is at this point that the careful recording of the actors' moves into the prompt copy by the DSM will be of vital importance. The director does not want to be in the dark about where on-stage an actor is standing at a particular moment that demands special lighting. If planning and recording of the rehearsals has gone well, then the lighting session plotting the lighting should go well. If there are delays, the director will learn from the producer and the theatre's chief executive exactly

what the phrase, 'Time is money', means! The director needs to know exactly what s/he wants to achieve, and will have to deploy maximum charm, discretion, determination and discipline to get it.

One very basic courtesy is to be sure of everyone's names and jobs from the venue. Another is to make sure that the statutory breaks are observed. As mentioned earlier, these seemingly insignificant matters can make an appreciative difference, particularly if time is running out and everyone has to pull together to hit the opening. Time will be different in a touring theatre. In a familiar, home theatre, where a company is resident or where it regularly plays, the director will know who to ask for any particular item or job. In the unfamiliar surroundings of a touring venue that is not necessarily the case. If this makes it sound as if touring theatres are difficult, that is not the intention: directors can feel

The character Wang in Brecht's *Good Soul of Szechuan*. Platform Theatre. The production setting was a closed library – a topical issue at the time. TRICIA DE COURCY LING

to visit the show on a regular basis – that could be as often as once a week or less often if a trusted stage manager is looking after the show. If it is a musical, it might have a nominated dance captain. Alternatively, there may be an assistant director touring with the show, playing a small role.

Keeping an Eye on the Show

Whatever the arrangements, the danger for a touring show is that the small additions and changes that naturally flow from a creative cast will, in the absence of the director's judgement about whether additions are positive or not, risk being in poor taste. The stage manager will write a show report after every show and it will be sent to the producer and the director every day; but even so it is quite possible that small changes can develop unnoticed. This is why the director needs to visit the show regularly to make sure the detail, as rehearsed, is maintained.

The other reason for the director to visit often is to keep an eye on the relationship between the people on tour. Away from home and with free days, it is very easy for a cast to fragment into cliques. At the very worst, strong feeling can to lead to misbehaviour. A cast of predominantly young men is particularly prone to get excited by rivalries, and need a careful eye. Mixed ages and mixed gender is less likely to cause problems. The director can help by being vigilant with notes; the regular, no-nonsense actors will take a poor view of a director who lets an actor get away with introducing improvised lines or stage business. The director must be rigorous in maintaining the quality of the show on tour. The remedy is, again, careful planning in logistics and in recruitment of the cast and the rest of the company who will be touring.

The warning above is nothing more than an alert. Most tours, of all kinds, give everyone a great time.

secure that touring venues are used to the routine of working fast and accurately. However, it is good to be aware that the experience is different on tour. (The fastest work schedule is in a rock venue. The crew do amazing things at incredible speed, because there is a lot of money tied up in the shows that are only on for one night.)

Having opened the show, it is likely that the director will stay for the second performance and give notes as usual. Depending on the set-up, and whether it is small-scale or a number one tour, the director's stay will be shorter or longer. Ideally, the director wants to leave the show after the opening in good, solid shape, with the cast, stage management and producer happy. At the end of the run at the first theatre, the set is packed up and the whole show moves on to the other venues. In a well-run set-up, the producer will want the director

REPLACEMENT CAST

When a play has been successful, it is very common to continue the run or the tour. The cast, however, will have been contracted for the initial period only. Very often some of the cast have to leave because they have taken on other work or they have proved to be disappointing, and some of the cast are ready to continue. Sometimes it is necessary to replace actors who have been disappointing.

The director has to re-audition (assuming there are no understudies) for those roles that are to be replaced. Re-rehearsing is very different from the initial rehearsal period. To begin with, the members of the cast who are staying will want to get the re-rehearsal out of the way as efficiently and as quickly as possible. Second, the producer or management will want to pay only what it costs to replace the people who have left; they do not want to pay for another rehearsal period. Third – and this is most important – it will not take anywhere near as long to put new people in to the production as the first rehearsal took.

The new actors might have had the opportunity to see the production and so come to the rehearsal with a good idea of the concept, as well as some of the detail, of the character they are going to play. Because other actors are staying, their characters will stay the same, so the dynamic between the newcomer and the old cast members will, in many respects, resemble what a previous actor did. The director will not want to say to the new actor, 'You're just going to imitate what went before', and so a game of bluff takes place where the new actor is allowed to make suggestions but, in the end, most of what went before is kept. Remember there are lighting cues, entrances and exits, position of furniture or the shape of the set: so the space to alter moves and character is very limited.

Because the remaining actors take up their rehearsed positions and speak their lines in a particular way, the incoming actor finds himself almost being steered around the set, and steered towards the interpretation of the role – it is as if the new actor will have to occupy the only empty space on the stage. This is why actors are sometimes reluctant to be part of a replacement cast. The director must keep everyone on point to adopt any new cast members and use the chance to freshen up the show. The director needs to make

Two charity collectors visit Scrooge. *A Christmas Carol*, Haymarket Theatre Basingstoke. ARNIM FREISS

The Spirit of Christmas Present and Scrooge visit the Cratchit family dinner. *A Christmas Carol*, Haymarket Theatre Basingstoke.
ARNIM FREISS

the replacement rehearsals fun and efficient, and treat the actors new to the production with extra care and courtesy, because it is very easy to make assumptions about a particular artistic decision when it has become embedded in the production.

REVIVALS

A revival of a show is different to a continuation with cast replacements. A complete revival will keep the original set and costume designs, but it will involve a new rehearsal period, which will not be as long as the original rehearsal period, but it will allow for changes and improvements. Some cast members will perhaps come back, but it is a chance for the director to learn from the previous run, and improve and edit the show, as necessary.

UNDERSTUDIES

The understudy is the poor relation of the main cast. S/he has to learn the lines and the moves and be ready to go on at a moment's notice. It is unlikely that s/he will get a proper rehearsal. Looking after the understudies is a job that the director can delegate to an assistant director, who will be very happy to have a specific responsibility.

Because each understudy will be covering several roles, however, the understudy rehearsal will not be complete. The director needs to be very attentive to the understudies; if things go wrong and there is an accident, the understudy is the insurance policy. The director should make sure s/he sees a run through with the understudies, because one of the reasons the understudies have agreed to it is because they hope to be seen by the director, and perhaps be cast in a more interesting capacity in the future. In a prestigious production of *Hamlet* at the Edinburgh Festival, Hamlet was suddenly taken ill. The understudy had not been properly rehearsed and was unable to go on, with the result that the producer lost money that evening. Even more importantly, the understudy actor lost a great opportunity to shine. The usual result is positive when an understudy has to go on – audiences rally round an understudy who comes up with the goods. Simon Russell Beale tripped and broke a finger in *Timon of Athens* at the National Theatre; it was announced he could not continue and there was a sad groan around the Olivier auditorium. When the understudy came on there was a thunderous round of applause and a huge ovation at the curtain call. This is why the star turn has to beware of his understudy!

Touring in the UK, and especially overseas, is one of the great consequential delights of working as a stage director. If offered, grab the opportunity!

11
TRAINING TO BECOME A DIRECTOR

TRAINING COURSES

How does a person start to be a director? It will be obvious from everything that has gone before that a major part of being a director is personality.

Liking people and plays are the guiding principles. The director also needs to appreciate actors' love of stories: reflected both in the stories of the plays and the love of stories in general, and the delight so many actors and other theatre people have in telling anecdotes. There is a Falstaff in every company of actors!

The question that confronts the would-be director is how to get started.

THE OLD WAY

The route taken by many of the directors, who, at the time of writing, are in their middle career, was to gain experience as an assistant director in a regional theatre. From the 1960s through to the late 1990s there was a network of about forty subsidized regional theatres. All major cities and very many towns had their own theatre buildings; a company of actors was recruited for the season (September to July), producing a mixed repertoire of plays. Very many actors, including Judy Dench and Ian McKellan, often speak of that system as the place where they grew up as actors. The same is true for several generations of directors.

Trevor Nunn (artistic director of the National Theatre) went from assistant director at Coventry Belgrade Theatre, while Richard Eyre was associate director at Edinburgh's Lyceum Theatre before Nottingham Playhouse and then the National Theatre. TV and film directors followed the same path. Many of the regional theatres also had a studio theatre attached, with a Theatre in Education team and, occasionally, a community

OPPOSITE: *Waiting for Godot*. The play with two tramps in which, famously, 'nothing happens, twice'. A trail-blazing, much copied, modern classic. Here, with Matthew Kelly as Vladimir.
ALISTAIR MUIR

RIGHT: *The Battle of Quiberon Bay*. An opera based on Handel's music. Bath International Music Festival, 2011.
ARNIM FREISS

SOME OF THE ESSENTIAL QUALITIES FOR A DIRECTOR

- Must like theatre and enjoy reading, watching and rehearsing plays. It sounds obvious but, strangely, some people who say they want to be directors do not enjoy theatre.
- Must have a love of language.
- Must have an interest in history and current affairs.
- Must like working in a social situation. Many talented people in the arts are very happy working on their own. Solo musicians, painters and novelists, are all creative working by themselves. Directors will be constantly with other people.
- Can understand the need to compromise, but can also identify and hold on to the essentials of their vision, when necessary.
- Does not expect to work office hours.
- Has something they want to contribute and communicate. It can be a desire to create joy or beauty, it can be to explore concepts of justice, it can be political, it can be educational – but the director *must* have something to say.
- Not in it for the money – if you are keen to make money there are much easier ways of doing it.

touring team. With a very high output of plays each season, the artistic director would need both associate and assistant directors. With directors frequently moving into TV and film, there was a very healthy climate for young directors to move up and flourish in.

A young person might have joined a theatre company in a junior capacity or as an actor, and at some later point, if he or she wanted to try directing, could ask the artistic director for a chance

OPPOSITE TOP: *The Saint of Bleeker Street*. The climax of the opera in the street. ARNIM FREISS

OPPOSITE BOTTOM: Oxford Stage Company's production of *Travesties* by Tom Stoppard. Stoppard's ingenious fantasy – a surreal, intellectual comedy. The kind of play that might well have had productions in regional repertory companies when they were producing seasons of their own work. This gave many opportunities to young directors. ALISTAIR MUIR

to direct a school's touring show or a Sunday evening one-off play reading. The financial cuts to theatres in the 1990s, together with the increased centralization of actors' careers in London, have effectively brought that system to an end.

A DIRECTING COURSE

There are a number of reputable directing courses in the UK.

One of the oldest established is at Drama Centre London, where a three-year BA course can be translated into an MA when the student takes a fourth year of study. The course puts the student director with acting students for much of the first year; the theory being that a director is better equipped to understand the actors' approach to rehearsal and performance if s/he has done some of the same training. In the second and third years there are increasing opportunities to direct scenes and eventually plays, as well as undertake secondments to professional companies. The fourth, MA year, is basically an academic year.

Among other options are one-year MA courses at drama schools like Bristol Old Vic School, LAMDA and East 15. Mountview Academy has a one-year MA course and, like other drama school courses, is able to offer directing students the chance of working with acting students in their scene studies and productions. At Bristol, students are expected to have some experience of directing other than student productions; and for an MA degree, a first-degree or equivalent is needed. There are other postgraduate courses at other drama schools.

University

Another route to training is through an MA at a university. The oldest established of these is at the University of East Anglia. Other universities offering an MA include Royal Holloway, University College Dublin and St Mary's College, Twickenham.

A university-based course will almost certainly include some element of academic work.

Another option is to take the part-time evening course in directing offered by the Royal Central School of Speech and Drama. Central also offers MA and MFA degrees through study in collaboration with other courses. The Royal Conservatoire of Scotland has a summer course as an introduction to directing. One great advantage that a university has over a drama school (or dedicated course) is that at university the student can try everything – acting, directing, writing, designing and producing – whereas an acting or a directing course is a very specialized training.

The reason the majority of the courses are at MA level is that most directors are drawn from individuals who have already had some practical theatre experience and are, therefore, older than the typical BA student. It is also true that for most young people interested in theatre, the practitioners who they have seen most often are actors. It is only after seeing a professional rehearsal or working as an actor or stage manager that most people see what a director actually does. Seeing a director at work can be the spur to wanting to take up directing as a career. It is worth remembering that it is very possible to do both – to act and direct, like Kenneth Branagh (indeed to write, act and direct like Harold Pinter). Artistic directors do still need assistants, so it is worth investigating that possibility with a local theatre, possibly as an intern.

FORMING A COMPANY

Following the decline of the regional repertory theatre network and the opportunities it offered to directors, there has been a huge growth in small, self-starter companies. As the funding for building-based companies started to fall away in the 1990s, directors started to make their own way, and continue to do so. Look at companies like Classics on a Shoestring, founded by, now internationally acclaimed director, Katie Mitchell in 1990 and Certain Dark Things, a company combining physical theatre, Commedia dell'Arte and puppetry, founded by Sarah Morgan in 2015. Both directors saw a gap in the market or had a strong intuition to start their own. Between these dates, literally hundreds of companies have been established, and continue to be born.

This development is exciting, but at the same time potentially daunting for a young director. The first thing to remember is that, at the beginning, it is not necessary to form a fully-fledged, legally incorporated company registered at Companies House. A director with a small group of actors, a designer, a good idea and a performance space is enough to start with. To be clear, from the start insurance must be put in place to cover any accidents to the audience or the performers. Later on you must, if you want to continue, get advice and go through all the legal requirements. It is a good idea to make any mistakes in a sheltered environment. The director should get two or three actors together and do a simple devised or existing text. The audience can be anyone – friends, family, old school or college – but it is important to have the experience of creating, producing and directing a show from the start to the finished production.

The director will know if s/he wants to continue after this first experimental stage. There are a number of sources, mainly on the internet, where people who have started their own companies have recorded their experiences. Here is list of the most important considerations:

1. Make sure you know why you are starting out on a very tough enterprise. There are already enough actors, directors and theatre companies in the world, so to make a success of starting a new company, the objectives must be absolutely clear. Work towards making a mission statement.
2. It will be the work that holds everything together, so that must be the priority, but not so much the priority that other important issues get relegated. The main other priority is money.
3. The finances of the company must be very carefully planned and constantly reviewed.

For an emerging company, unless there is an angel willing to risk financially underpinning the whole enterprise (unlikely), the members will have to take part-time jobs. Obviously, it is more rewarding if those jobs are in some way related to theatre or the arts more generally, but the overriding consideration is that the whole group make themselves available for rehearsals. It is advisable to create a timetable for how future financing will operate. For example, to rely on day jobs for two years; after that to pay each company member for performances, while still working during the day; after four years to become a full-time, fully financed company.

4. All small companies will aspire to apply for Arts Council funding, but these days that is so remote for start-up companies that looking for other sources will definitely be more successful. Investigate the possibility of raising funds by your company doing performances associated with social issues, public health, conference and corporate work, where there might be other sources of funding.

5. Like an emerging rock band, the pressure of keeping everyone together is immense – which is why it is prudent not to have too large a number of people in the company.

6. The work is the central, unique aspect of the company. What is new and interesting about it? The kind of plays of which many actors are fond – Chekhov, Strindberg, Shakespeare – would be competing in a very crowded market. Complicité has had enormous success with its pioneering approach to performance. On close examination, most of the justifiably famous companies got to their reputation by being adventurous. What is more likely to attract attention – a small company performing Shakespeare sonnets or a small company using music, movement, comedy and text in a performance examining the threats and dangers of the internet? The name of the company should capture the aims and interests of the company. Shared Experience, Complicité, Northern Broadsides and National Theatre of Brent, all give a hint of the kind of way in which they want the audience to think of them.

7. Think of selling the inherent skills of the company to other markets – like corporate presentation and public speaking courses. There is an increasing interest in using theatre skills in many areas of training and teaching, such as the police, the legal and the medical professions.

8. Be very secure on the administration. Banking arrangements can be tedious but have to be done. A group of actors and a director are probably not going to prioritize administration over artistic concerns, but administration is the scaffolding that supports the artistic structure and must not be let slip. Decide how the company will be run. If founded by a director, then s/he should run it. If a group of equals, then sometimes a working democracy can work, though it is often sorely tested.

9. Identify the audience/market. Investigate the other companies working in the same area. What is the selling point of the new company? Who is the audience in demographic and geographic terms? Is that part of the market already catered for and is there room for another contender? What is the brand of the new company? Find partnerships with other organizations. Not necessarily arts' organizations, but outfits who work in other spheres to whom you can offer benefits. There might be a space that you can rent cheaply in return for putting on a show for local seniors.

10. Discipline is paramount. The director needs to exercise exemplary leadership skills and to ensure that every aspect of the work is properly attended to.

11. Enjoy the ride! The point about theatre is that no-one makes a lot of money (apart from a very tiny number of very lucky actors and the very occasional director). If the director and actors do not have fun, what is the point? There are more comfortable ways of not earning much!

Women in Benjamin Britten's *The Rape of Lucretia* at the Dartington International Summer School and Festival. ARNIM FREISS

Directors come from a wide variety of backgrounds; some with a long history of performance and others just starting out on their careers. Either way there will be a larger or smaller reservoir of plays read, seen or performed, which can serve as the basis of a director's repertoire. The director can use the strength of previous reviews to try and persuade a theatre or company to revive the production. There is a great premium placed on being original, and while it is important to have a unique feel to a production, it is also legitimate – and necessary – to stand on the shoulders of giants. Offer imitation as the sincerest form of flattery.

To finish on a personal note again. I started out running the marketing for theatre, and loved designing the posters and programmes and finding new audiences. I acted for a time and that was very fulfilling, but directing has most certainly given me the most satisfaction. My long time as a stage director has given me a wonderful career. I have met many interesting and extraordinary people, and been put into endless odd and amusing situations. I have felt at times like a formal, well-dressed businessman, and at other times like an old fashioned Bohemian. I have sometimes had to attempt to be a politician in defence of a theatre company, and sometimes had to duck and dive to achieve a memorable production. I don't feel I've worked, in the conventional sense of the word, for one day! I hope this book helps anyone who wants to try this multi-layered, creative and daring adventure.

The characters in *Waiting for Godot* are grounded! Oxford Stage Company production. ALISTAIR MUIR

The Fool and King Lear, Everyman, Liverpool production with Antony Sher as the Fool. CAROL BAUGH

APPENDIX:
TWENTY THINGS FOR A
DIRECTOR TO DO

1. Go to art exhibitions. In London: National Gallery, National Portrait Gallery, Tate Britain, Tate Modern and The Wallace Collection. Catch a tour by one of the curators. If not in London, visit the numerous excellent regional galleries, e.g. Tate Liverpool and Tate St Ives, Walker Art Gallery, Manchester Gallery, Edinburgh's Scottish National Gallery and the Gallery of Modern Art, Glasgow.
2. Go to classical music concerts. In London: The Barbican Centre, The South Bank Centre or The Royal Albert Hall for the proms. Pop music is pretty well covered for most people. If not in London, visit a local music society or one of the regional concert halls with a visiting orchestra.
3. Read the arts' reviews in a reputable newspaper every day, e.g. *The Guardian*, *The Times* or *The Telegraph*. WhatsOnStage is a reputable website.
4. See an opera: English National Opera, Royal Opera, Opera North, Welsh National, Scottish National or one of the smaller companies like English Touring Opera and La Serenissima.
5. See a classical and a contemporary ballet: English National Ballet, Royal Ballet, Ballet Rambert, Akram Khan, Michael Clark and London Contemporary Dance.
6. Go to a professional football match, e.g. your local team.
7. Keep abreast of political events. Go canvassing for a political party.
8. Visit a cathedral or other religious building.
9. Read history books and watch the History Channel and BBC 4.
10. Go to drama schools' final shows.
11. Go to play readings.
12. Look at extracts from famous performances on YouTube.
13. Visit castles and stately homes.
14. Go to the theatre every week.
15. Organize a personal website.
16. Learn to read music.
17. Go up for a part in a play and be auditioned.
18. Be relentlessly curious about everything.
19. Learn to dance – waltz, tango, salsa.
20. Take a course in leadership and communication from a reputable company. The company Improve on You is particularly good with directors.

GLOSSARY

THE BUILDING

Black Box Theatre A room (often painted black) that is intended for performance and lacks a permanent configuration, seating or fixed performance area. Provision for performance lighting and props or a curtain is often made.

Fringe Theatre An *ad hoc* performance space.

Theatre A place for the exhibition of dramatic, musical or dance performances for an audience.

THE PHYSICAL STAGE

Apron The usually curved area of the stage closest to the audience.

Backdrop The drop farthest upstage in most settings; also, a large curtain, sometimes with a picture or design.

Backstage Usually the entire stage area not visible to the audience.

Cyclorama (or Cyc) A large, usually white, curtain that is lit to create setting, and masks the back of the stage behind the set.

Fly Tower The area above the stage where curtains and set pieces are stored and hidden during a production.

Front of House The part of the theatre that accommodates the audience, including the foyer, the stalls, the dress circle, the royal circle and the highest tier of seats, the upper circle, informally known as 'The Gods'.

Legs Narrow curtains in the wings to mask the backstage areas.

Off-Stage Any area that is onstage but not in view of the audience.

Orchestra Pit A lower area between the stage and audience seating area where the musicians sit, so the audience can hear the music and see the performance over the heads of the musicians.

Proscenium An arched opening through which the audience sees the stage; also, a style of theatre with the audience seated predominantly in front of the stage (also informally referred to as 'the pros').

Raked Stage or 'Rake' A sloped platform that is lower near the audience for better visibility and higher at the rear, providing the illusion of distance. This is the source for the terms 'downstage' and 'upstage'.

Studio Space A theatre space designed where the seating arrangements can be changed and altered for each production, to suit the artistic vision of the director.

The Curtain The front, often decorative, curtain of a stage; also, called 'The Tabs'.

The House The audience area; also, this expression is often used to describe the make-up and response of the audience, i.e. full house, good house, thin house, quiet house.

The Safety Curtain Line/The Iron A sheet of iron that is dropped in front of the curtain to prevent the spread of a possible fire. This is in place before a performance, brought down in-between acts and dropped in at the end of the show.

Thrust Where the stage or part of the stage comes out into the auditorium.

Trap An opening in the stage floor for actors to pass through making entrances and exits.

Traverse Where the stage is positioned with the audience either side of the performance space.

Wings The areas to the left and right of the stage, out of view to the audience.

REHEARSAL/PRODUCTION

Auditions Interviews and readings before a director, to determine casting of a play.

Band Call/*Sitzprobe* The first rehearsal of songs with the full orchestra.

Come Down In the theatre, a show does not finish, it 'comes down', i.e. the curtain 'comes down' to end the show. An actor might ask, 'What time do we come down?'.

Corpse When an actor who gets an unintended and uncontrollable fit of laughter on stage s/he is said to 'corpse'.

Costumes The clothing worn by the actors that helps determine character, time, theme and mood.

Curtain Call/Bows The choreographed appearance of actors on stage after the performance to acknowledge the applause of the audience.

Curtain Up The start of the performance.

Dark A time when all lights are out or the theatre is closed.

Dialogue Written conversation.

Die When a show is said to 'die' it only has a short, unsuccessful run and will usually have received poor reviews.

Dress Rehearsal The final run of the show with all elements in place – props, lights, sound, costume and orchestra.

Exposition The explanation of who, what, when, where and why of a play.

First Night The first public performance with the press in attendance.

Go Up In the theatre a show does not 'start' *per se* but 'goes up' as in, 'What time does the curtain go up?'.

Heads! A term of warning used to call attention to overhead danger.

Improvise To extemporise around an idea or theme of the play.

Initial Incident The first most important event in a play from which the rest of the play develops.

Notes When the director calls all the actors together to give out notes and observations on the rehearsal s/he has just seen. Often called a notes' session.

Notice Given when a production is to be closed down.

Off Book When the actor has learnt his/her lines and is ready to rehearse without carrying the script.

Places The direction for all actors, musicians and technicians to go to their proper position and be ready for the beginning of a play or scene.

Practical Adjective used to describe properties or scenery that have to work as in real life when used, e.g. a practical ceiling light must actually light up when switched on by an actor.

Previews Public performances that are put on before the press night of a show – usually at a reduced pricing. During previews, many changes are often made to fine-tune the performance.

Props Small hand-held items used by actors to create the period, character or setting.

Recall An additional audition for the final actors being considered.

Run Through An uninterrupted rehearsal of a scene, act or the entire play.

Script A complete scene or play in a format to be produced by actors and directors.

Sightlines The area of the stage that can be seen by everyone seated in the auditorium. A director will have to be mindful of sightlines if one actor is blocking another or an actor places him/herself in an obscured part of the stage.

Stage Manager Person responsible for the physical set-up, actors and technical cues of a production as it is performed.

Strike Taking down and putting away costumes, props and sets after a production.

Technical Rehearsal A staggered walk through of the show onstage to give the technical crew an opportunity to plot sound, focus lights and run all technical elements of a production.

The Half Thirty-five minutes before curtain up, when all people associated with the performance must be in the building.

Workshop A period of rehearsal designed to explore the first draft of a script. While there may be a 'sharing' at the end of this period, there is no formal performance.

THE ELEMENTS OF THE PLAY

Act An organizational division in scripts.

Antagonist This character forces change or creates conflict for the protagonist.

Climax The major event in a play, the turning point of the story.

Conclusion The final outcome of the play.

Falling Action/Denouement The series of events following the climax.

Monologue A long speech said by a single actor to himself or herself, the audience or to another character.

Protagonist The play revolves around this character.

Rising Action The series of events following the initial incident; how the story builds towards its climax.

Scene An organizational division in scripts marking out separate parts of the story.

Setting Where the play occurs in terms of time and place.

Soliloquy A long speech said by a single actor to himself or herself or the audience, but not to another character.

Theme/Message/Purpose/Moral What the play, as a piece of art, is trying to say to the audience.

ACTOR'S TERMINOLOGY

Ad Lib Lines made up by an actor to fill in where there would be an undesirable pause due to missed or forgotten lines, technical problems, etc.

Aside Lines said to the audience that other actors onstage are not supposed to be hearing.

Build To increase the tempo or volume or both to reach a climax in a scene.

Business Small actions, such as smoking, using a fan, pouring a drink, etc., used to fill time, to create character and sometimes to make the action 'more realistic'.

Cast The actors taking the various roles in a production.

Cue The last words or actions indicating the time for another actor to speak or move.

Diction The actor's ability to be understood by the audience.

Doubling When an actor takes on more than one role in any specific production.

Focus Where the director wants the audience to look – the actor's point of concentration.

Mime A story or action performed without words relying on body language.

Open Up/Cheat Out Facing as much towards the audience as possible.

Pick-Up Cues A direction for the actor to begin responding immediately without allowing any lapsed time.

Principal Players Those actors taking leading roles.

Take the Stage What an actor does when they take control of the scene or take the focus of the audience.

To Dry (verb) When an actor forgets their lines.

To Upstage (verb) When one actor moves upstage of another, forcing the other actor to look upstage and away from the audience – considered very bad practice.

Understudy An actor playing a small part in a production, who will cover various roles in the play and go on, should another actor be indisposed.

Volume The actor's ability to be heard by the audience.

RECOMMENDED READING

Bogdanov, M., *Shakespeare, The Director's Cut* (Capercaillie Books Limited, 2013)
A blizzard of ideas. A great read.

Bradby, D. and Williams, D., *Directors' Theatre* (Macmillan, 1982)
A detailed summary of one American and six prestigious European directors, including Peter Brook, Joan Littlewood and Robert Wilson. Detailed analysis of individual productions.

Braun, E., *The Director and the Stage* (Methuen, 1982)
A basic text book – detailed, academic study of directing from Naturalism to Grotowski.

Caird, J., *Theatre Craft; A Director's Practical Companion from A to Z* (Faber and Faber, 2010)
A very practical and easy to read compendium.

Calderone, M. and Lloyd-Williams, M., *Actions: the Actors' Thesaurus* (Nick Herne Books, 2004)
This is an essential directory for a director who is using actioning.

Donnellan, D., *The Actor and the Target* (Nick Hern Books, 2002)
His fresh and radical approach to acting explained.

Hagen, U. and Frankel, H., *Respect for Acting* (Wiley Publishing, 1991)
Primarily for actors; describes how to put Stanislavski's system into day-to-day use.

Johnstone, K., *Impro: Improvisation and the Theatre* (Methuen, 1982)
The grandaddy of improvisation. Very entertaining, but seminal and readable.

McGrath, J., *A Good Night Out* (Eyre Methuen, 1981)
Looks at different ways different classes take their entertainment and surveys Brecht and 7:84.

Mamet, D., *True and False: Heresy and Common Sense for the Actor* (Faber and Faber, 1998)
An invigorating counter-blast to Stanislavski's system.

Murray, B., *How to Direct a Play* (Oberon Books, 2011)
A personal view of directing with lots of anecdotes.

Stanislavski, K., *My Life in Art* (Routledge, 2008)
The great originator of the system. An easier read than anticipated.

Swain, R., *Directing. A Handbook for Emerging Theatre Directors* (Bloomsbury, 2011)
A comprehensive description of his experience running a training course at Birkbeck College. Lots of good detail.

Usher, S., *Directing, A Miscellany* (Oberon Books, 2014)
A little book of perceptive reflections, questions and maxims on life as a director. Occasionally oblique, but always thoughtful and interesting.

Williams, D., *Peter Brook, A Theatrical Casebook* (Methuen, 1998)
An expert reconstruction of a dozen of Brook's major works.

There are many other books on various aspects of directing, but directing is really learnt by doing it, and watching and thinking about what happens in the rehearsal room and on stage.

INDEX